MIGHTIER
Than the
SWORD

Rebels, Reformers, and
Revolutionaries Who Changed the
World Through Writing

by Rochelle Melander
illustrated by Melina Ontiveros

For the Dream Keepers
who are already changing the world through writing

27 26 25 24 23 22 21   1 2 3 4 5 6 7 8

Hardcover ISBN: 978-1-5064-6640-8
Ebook ISBN: 978-1-5064-6891-4

Library of Congress Cataloging-in-Publication Data
Names: Melander, Rochelle, author. | Ontiveros, Melina, illustrator.
Title: Mightier than the sword : rebels, reformers, and revolutionaries who changed the world through writing /
    by Rochelle Melander ; illustrations by Melina Ontiveros.
Description: Minneapolis, MN : Beaming Books, an imprint of 1517 Media, 2021. | Includes bibliographical references.
    | Audience: Ages 9-13 | Summary: "Interactive and inspiring, Mightier Than the Sword celebrates the stories of over
    forty diverse, trailblazing people whose writing transformed history"-- Provided by publisher.
Identifiers: LCCN 2020056542 (print) | LCCN 2020056543 (ebook) | ISBN 9781506466408 (hardcover) |
    ISBN 9781506468914 (ebook)
Subjects: LCSH: Biography--Juvenile literature.
Classification: LCC CT107 .M48 2021 (print) | LCC CT107 (ebook) | DDC 920--dc23
LC record available at https://lccn.loc.gov/2020056542
LC ebook record available at https://lccn.loc.gov/2020056543

CPSIA: VN0004589; 9781506466408; MAY2021

Beaming Books
510 Marquette Avenue
Minneapolis, MN 55402
Beamingbooks.com

Table of Contents

Introduction

If a song has inspired you or a book has changed the way you think, you know that words can transform.

If you've written a thank-you note or received a kind text from a friend, you know that words can make a difference.

If you've won a verbal argument or been hurt by a classmate's jab, you know the power of words.

British author Edward Bulwer-Lytton said, "The pen is mightier than the sword." French ruler and military leader Napoleon Bonaparte fought with swords in multiple battles and still believed, he said, "Four hostile newspapers are more to be feared than a thousand bayonets." But these men weren't the first to proclaim the power of words over weapons. In the seventh century BCE, the Assyrian sage Ahiqar taught, "The word is mightier than the sword."

Many people have put this adage into action, writing books, giving speeches, and even tweeting to spread their message. In November 2010, a teen named Rene Silva tweeted to help the world understand how a drug war between police and drug traffickers was affecting the lives of ordinary people in Rio de Janeiro, Brazil.

In 2010, the government issued an ultimatum to the drug traffickers who ruled the streets of Rene's neighborhood: surrender or we will invade. Two days later, soldiers marched into the community carrying rifles and setting fire to buses. The drug dealers fled to the hills.

As the world watched this nightmare unfold on television and Twitter, Rene and his fellow teenage correspondents told the whole story through tweets. While machine gunfire exploded around him, seventeen-year-old student journalist Rene sat in his grandmother's tiny house, tweeting from a PC:

"Intense gunfire now in Complexo"

"People hanging out white cloths calling for peace"

"The pizza shop is closed! Saturday night isn't Saturday night without pizza!"

When Rene was eleven years old, he had founded a monthly newspaper called *Voz da Comunidade* (*The Voice of the Community*) to share news about the problems in his community. Tweeting helped him reach a whole new audience. By the end of the siege, Rene's Twitter account had grown from 180 to 20,000 followers. Today, his account has 377,000 followers. He has spoken around the world and was named one of the 100 Most Influential People of African Descent (MIPAD) under age 40.

Throughout history, people have written to protest injustice, preserve culture, and imagine new futures. Young people and adults have risked their reputations and lives to propose scientific theories, declare independence, and start revolutions. Their words have changed minds, freed enslaved people, and legislated equality.

This book tells their stories.

Because your story matters too, each chapter includes a writing activity. You can write about the experiences, ideas, and causes you care about.

The minute you put pen to paper, you change. When you share your writing, it changes others. Your words have the power to transform you and your world.

Take up your pen and write!

Murasaki Shikibu

Novelist, 978–1016

Write to Invent:
The Tale of Genji

When she was a little girl, Murasaki Shikibu stood by the door, listening in on her brother's Chinese lessons. The government forbade girls from learning the official language, literary Chinese. But her reading and writing skills quickly surpassed her brother's, causing her father to say, "Just my luck! What a pity she was not born a man!"

Raised by a father who wrote poetry, Murasaki learned to do calligraphy, play music, and write Japanese verse. After marrying and having a daughter, Murasaki did something no one had ever done before: she wrote a novel.

Two years after Murasaki married, her husband died of cholera. She wrote stories to cope with her sadness. Empress Shōshi invited her to be her lady-in-waiting. Murasaki taught her Chinese and read her stories, including episodes from her novel *The Tale of Genji*. Once, after she read a story, someone called her the "Lady of the Chronicles" and spread rumors that Murasaki was flaunting her learning. Later, after being caught reading Chinese books that had been wasting away in the cupboard, someone said, "What kind of lady is it who reads Chinese books?"

Murasaki lashed out in her diary. At public parties, it was common to invite guests to recite a poem on the spot. Murasaki wrote, "People who think so much of themselves that they will, at the drop of a hat, compose lame verses that only just hang together, or produce the most pretentious compositions imaginable, are quite odious and rather pathetic."

Before Murasaki wrote *The Tale of Genji*, people wrote poems, stories, and longer narratives that incorporated fantasy or fairy tales. Instead, Murasaki filled her novel with realistic romantic and political scenes. Her story reminds readers that we live with the "sadness of things" (a phrase she used over a thousand times).

The Tale of Genji was written long before the invention of the printing press, and it was copied by hand. One teenager read a tale from the novel and "longed for the rest," writing in her diary, "I was all impatience and yearning, and in my mind was always praying that I might read all the books of Genji-monogatari from the very first one."

Recognized as one of the greatest works of Japanese literature, *The Tale of Genji* contains fifty-four chapters and is 750,000 words long. (That's about three thousand double-spaced pages!) The story has had a huge impact on Japanese culture. The novel inspired artists and calligraphers to craft scenes from the novel on screen paintings, hanging scrolls, and lacquered boxes.

Because Murasaki wrote her book in kana, a sort of phonetic Chinese, it helped develop Japanese into a written language. In the twelfth century, people began writing fan fiction. Writers have adapted the story into plays, novels, movies, and comic books. Now more than one thousand years old, *The Tale of Genji* remains required (and desired) reading all over the world.

WRITE TO KNOW

Japanese writers used a form of poetry called waka or tanka, which is like a sonnet. The tanka starts with three lines (5/7/5 syllables). Then *whoosh!*— the feeling changes—and the last two lines express the shift (7/7 syllables). (Look familiar? Years later, poets wrote just the first stanza, and called it haiku.)

WRITE NOW

How do you communicate with friends and family? In Murasaki's time, people exchanged poetry. Create a tanka poem to describe a dramatic event to a friend.

WRITE TO CREATE: THE MASHUP NOVEL

The term *mashup* originated in the music industry: musicians combine two songs to make a new composition. In her novel, Murasaki combined several types of literature, including Chinese histories and narrative poetry. Today writers take elements from a classic novel, like the characters and plot, and mash them up with a different genre. What kind of mashup story would you create?

Had **Sei Shonagon (965–1010)** lived today, she might have created the first etiquette guide or developed a social sharing site like Instagram. Sei captured court life in *The Pillow Book*, a genre known as zuihitsu that combined lists, advice on conversation and letter writing, observations about events, and suggestions on clothing.

Wicked, indeed, to write so much of others!

—*Murasaki Shikibu*

Abu Abdullah Muhammad Ibn Battuta

Traveler, 1304–1377

Write to Chronicle: *Rihla (The Travels):
A Gift to Those Who Contemplate the
Wonders of Cities and the Marvels of
Traveling*

Twenty-one-year-old Abu Abdullah Muhammad Ibn Battuta had just finished his law studies in his hometown of Tangier, Morocco, when he set out on his first hajj, a pilgrimage to Mecca, Islam's holiest city. Ibn Battuta's search for spiritual enlightenment led him on a journey that lasted thirty years, covered 73,000 miles, and included visits to more than forty-four modern-day countries.

Ibn Battuta knew that to be a faithful Muslim he must complete a hajj at least once in his lifetime. But it wasn't easy to leave his home. He wrote:

Swayed by an overmastering impulse within me, and a long-cherished desire to visit those glorious sanctuaries, I resolved to quit all my friends and tear myself away from my home.

Ibn Battuta traveled alone on a donkey. But it wasn't safe. Bandits lined the route, waiting to rob travelers. Shortly after he joined a caravan of pilgrims, the summer heat overtook the party and everyone got sick. After resting for ten days, they traveled on. Then Ibn Battuta came down with a fever but was determined to continue. He tied himself to his saddle to keep from falling off his donkey. About this incident he wrote, "If God decrees my death, it shall be on the road with my face set toward Mecca."

As the pilgrims arrived in the next city, people came to greet them. Ibn Battuta knew no one and was consumed by grief: "I was so affected by my loneliness that I could not restrain my tears and wept bitterly." Most people return home after visiting Mecca, especially if they're homesick. But Ibn Battuta had a dream about riding on the wing of a large bird to Mecca, Yemen, and other countries and took this as a sign. Instead of heading home, he set out to explore the Muslim world.

Over the course of his life, Ibn Battuta made the pilgrimage to Mecca at least six times. He studied Sufism, a form of Islam in which believers connect to God through poetry, music, and dance. He learned from spiritual teachers and became friends with scholars, officials, merchants, kings, and Muslim leaders. He often bumped into people he knew on the road. Because of Muslim rules of hospitality, Ibn Battuta could depend on receiving lodging, food, and gifts from fellow Muslims on his journey.

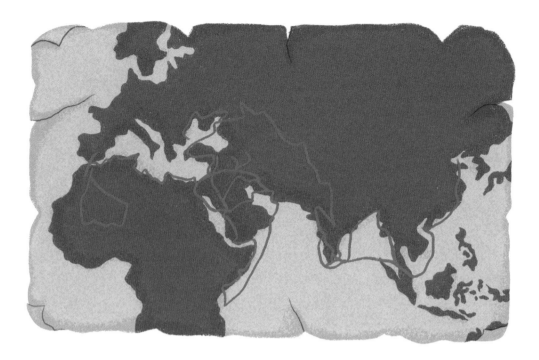

During his travels, Ibn Battuta was kidnapped, was robbed, nearly drowned in a ship accident, and almost died from eating yams. He took breaks and studied law, worked as a judge and ambassador, married at least ten times, and had several children.

When he returned home in 1354, Ibn Battuta dictated his story to Ibn Juzayy, recording vivid descriptions of the people and places he'd encountered in his travels. His memoirs provide a remarkable view of fourteenth-century Islamic life, travel practices, and the landscapes, plants, and animals of the time.

WRITE TO KNOW

Ibn Battuta depended on the advice of fellow travelers to navigate his journey. Today, professional travelers create online guides to help people discover the best places to see, eat, and stay. Tourists contribute tips and reviews. Here's what you might find in a travel guide:

- Destinations and their history, geography, culture, and climate
- Basic advice on
  - when to go
  - how to get there and get around
  - where to eat and sleep
  - where to buy supplies and souvenirs
- Trip itineraries based on
  - themes (Jazz Age! Yarn making!)
  - interests (Baseball! Shell seeking!)
  - time (Day trips! Weekend getaways!)

When **Isabella Bird (1831–1904)** became ill as an adult, her doctor prescribed travel. Isabella felt healthier when she explored unfamiliar places, met new people, and wrote about them. Her book *The Yangtze Valley and Beyond* smashed prejudices about China and its people.

WRITE NOW

What places do you wish you could share with others? Write a travel guide to a beloved place in your home or community. Or go tiny, and lead the reader through a beehive, a motherboard, or the digestive system. Make a map to help travelers find their way.

Traveling—it leaves you speechless, then turns you into a storyteller.

—*Abu Abdullah Muhammad Ibn Battuta*

Martin Luther

Theologian, 1483–1546

Write to Debate: "Ninety-Five Theses: Disputation on the Power and Efficacy of Indulgences"

On his way back to law school, Martin Luther was caught in a violent thunderstorm. Terrified, he vowed to St. Anne that if he survived, he would enter a monastery and devote his life to God.

Martin's father was furious—he wanted his son to become a lawyer. He asked, "What if that was the devil calling you?" Still, Martin trusted God's call. He led the monks and taught biblical studies at the university in Wittenberg, Germany.

But Martin worried he could never do enough to please God. He wasn't alone. Many people feared being sent to purgatory after death, a place where it was believed suffering erased the effects of sin and prepared people to be with God in heaven. Church leaders took advantage of this fear by selling indulgences, pieces of paper that represented good works and that leaders claimed released a person from spending time in purgatory.

Martin feared that the people who purchased indulgences might lose faith, become lazy or reckless, and that God would judge them and send them to purgatory anyway. He wrote about these concerns to his archbishop.

Martin didn't wait for a response—people's souls were at stake! He wrote what became known as the "Ninety-Five Theses," a list of points for debate centered on two key ideas: First, the Bible is the main religious authority—not the pope or bishops. Second, salvation comes to people as a free gift of God via their faith. Indulgences weren't necessary.

In Martin's day, people posted notices on church doors to announce public events. Legend has it that Martin nailed his "Ninety-Five Theses" to the door of the Castle Church in Wittenberg on October 31, 1517. In reality, Martin probably pasted his theses—the typical method for hanging notices—to many church doors that night. Then Martin scheduled a debate.

No one showed up. And that might have been the end of the story, if Martin's theses hadn't gone viral. Martin sent copies to friends, someone translated his Latin words into German, printers published copies, and the theses quickly spread across the country.

Martin also wrote "Sermon on Indulgences and Grace" in German and published the pamphlet. It became a bestseller and reprinted fourteen times in 1518, in print runs of one thousand copies. This publication ignited the Reformation, the religious and political challenge to the pope and the Catholic Church in Europe. The Reformation led to the creation of many Protestant churches.

The leaders of the Catholic Church excommunicated Martin. The emperor issued an edict, banning Martin's writings and demanding his arrest. Anyone who fed or sheltered the monk would be breaking the law. But killing Martin? That would be okay.

Fearing for Martin's life, the ruler Frederick the Wise had him kidnapped and taken to Wartburg Castle. In his eleven weeks in hiding, Martin translated the New Testament into German. Martin's translation made it possible for ordinary people to read the Bible.

In addition to changing the theology of the church, Martin's writings also helped unify the German language and improved the literacy of the German people. His Bible and pamphlets were read aloud and debated at dinner tables, in taverns, and at spinning bees. To spread the message, Martin and his supporters set religious lyrics to popular folk songs, creating hymns and ballads that people enjoyed singing. Martin wrote so much that in the first half of the sixteenth century, he'd written more than a third of all books published in German!

The scholar **William Tyndale (1494–1536)** was the first person to translate the Bible into English from the original Hebrew and Greek. He introduced new words and phrases, and modern English translations still rely on his work. William was declared a heretic and burned at the stake.

If you want to change the world, pick up your pen and write.

—*Martin Luther*

WRITE TO KNOW

Johannes Gutenberg (1400–1468) developed a system to mass-produce text using movable type. In 1455, he created an edition of the Latin Bible that became popular for its readability. The process that produced the Gutenberg Bible made it possible to easily print text for the public, increasing literacy and contributing to the growth of the European Renaissance and the Reformation.

WRITE NOW

Martin Luther wrote the "Ninety-Five Theses" to invite debate and prompt change. What do you care about so much that you could write your own ninety-five theses? Write it!

How will you invite debate? Post your ideas on social media? Hold a poetry slam? Make a music video?

WRITE TO CREATE

Martin Luther used repetition and rhythm so people would enjoy reading his words aloud. He used relatable images to explain complex topics: "A lie is like a snowball: the further you roll it, the bigger it becomes." Keep a notebook to record juicy words, favorite phrases, and interesting snippets of conversation.

William Shakespeare

**Playwright and Poet,
1564–1616**

Write to Dramatize:
Romeo and Juliet

If you've eaten "too much of a good thing" or worried about becoming a "laughingstock," thank William Shakespeare. If you've stared at your homework and said, "It's Greek to me"—you're quoting the Bard (William's nickname). Shakespeare wrote 884,647 words in thirty-eight plays, two narrative poems, and 154 sonnets. Although his characters sometimes sound like they're spouting sonnets, William tried to include more prose in his plays. The fancy language? That's just how people talked!

William Shakespeare dropped out of school when he was thirteen, probably to earn money for his family. He became a teenage father after marrying the pregnant Anne Hathaway. Seven years later, the father of three was living in London, acting, writing plays, and managing Lord Chamberlain's Men. He

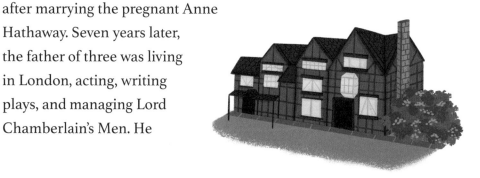

went home to Stratford-upon-Avon every year for Lent, when the theaters were closed.

Despite his lack of formal education, William knew the classics and read contemporary literature. He borrowed plots, characters, and themes from the Bible and writers like Geoffrey Chaucer. He quoted phrases and passages from current plays, poems, history books, and stories in his work. But this wasn't considered plagiarism. In William's day, people valued the skill of retelling popular tales—and William made it an art form.

William's company performed his plays at outdoor theaters, mostly in the afternoon. People ate, drank, and chatted through the performances. Women were forbidden from performing, so all of the actors were men. Young boys played the women's roles.

Although Queen Elizabeth enjoyed attending plays, not everyone believed theater was a moral pastime. Civic leaders thought playgoers were slackers, seeing plays to shirk work. A London preacher proclaimed, "The cause of plagues is sin, and the cause of sin is plays—therefore the cause of plagues are plays." But others praised the theater for distracting people from gambling and drinking. (Didn't they know that audience members guzzled ale while cheering for the heroes and booing the villains?)

The bubonic plague plagued William's life. Shortly after he was born, it killed a quarter of the population in his small hometown. Between 1603 and 1613, the plague forced London playhouses to close for a total of seventy-eight months. During one outbreak, William wrote *King Lear* and *Macbeth*, and polished *Anthony and Cleopatra*. William also put the plague in his plays, having a character in *Romeo and Juliet* declare, "A plague on both your houses!"

Critics wondered how an ordinary bloke like William—who didn't have royal blood, wasn't part of the nobility, and never graduated from university—could write with such deep insight into humanity. In a 1592 article, the London playwright Robert Greene wrote, "There is an upstart Crow . . . supposes he is as well able to bombast out a blank verse as the best of you."

Not everyone felt that way. Friend and fellow writer Ben Jonson said this of William: "He was not of an age but for all time!" Indeed, William's poems and plays have inspired readers for more than four hundred years. His work has endured because people can relate to the characters, events, and themes. William told stories of people falling in love, suffering, plotting revenge, wrestling with good and evil, and changing their lives.

American composer and playwright **Lin-Manuel Miranda (1980–)** got inspiration from William Shakespeare's plays when he wrote his epic historical musical *Hamilton*. In the song "Take a Break," Lin-Manuel used these words from *Macbeth*: "Tomorrow and tomorrow and tomorrow / Creeps in this petty pace from day to day."

Sigmund Freud (1856–1939), founder of psychoanalysis, used William's stories to help people understand how humans function. South African president Nelson Mandela (1918–2013) kept a copy of *The Complete Works of Shakespeare* by his bedside. Writers have borrowed stories and characters from William's work to create novels, films, musicals, poems, and paintings. As William would say, "All's well that ends well."

WRITE NOW

William Shakespeare wrote comedies, tragedies, and histories. What story do you want to tell? Create your own skit or one-act play on a theme that matters to you. Borrow characters or the plot from an existing play—maybe even one of Shakespeare's!

WRITE TO CREATE

William Shakespeare invented more than four hundred words and phrases to make his point and reach the people of his day. Here are some examples of how William crafted words. Create your own.

CHANGED NOUNS AND NAMES INTO VERBS:

"She Phebes me."

"Come, sermon me no further."

"Disorder, that hath spoil'd us, friend us now!"

ADDED A PREFIX:

Import

Outdare

Oversize

COMBINED WORDS:

Made-up

Leapfrog

Wormhole

INVENTED WORDS:

Buzzer

Zany

Zounds

Shakespeare wrote fabulous insults, like this line from *Henry IV*: "Thou leathern-jerkin, crystal-button, knot-pated, agatering, puke-stocking, caddis-garter, smooth-tongue, Spanish pouch!"

Suit the action to the word, the word to the action.

—*William Shakespeare*

Write to Film:
Screenplays

When the going gets tough, the tough get going—to the movies. And why not? Where else can you escape reality to journey under the sea, over the rainbow, or to a galaxy far, far away? Only in your dreams! That's why the first moviegoers called theaters "dream palaces." But films also give us something a dream can't: a shared experience.

The first movies were silent black-and-white stories that lasted less than a minute. For these films, screenwriters composed a scenario, a summary of the story that the company used to shoot and promote the film. The Edison film catalog featured this scenario for the short film *Blanket-Tossing a New Recruit*: "Company F, 1st Ohio Volunteers, initiating a new man. Nineteen times he bounces in the blanket, and each toss is funnier than the last one."

For silent films, writers created "intertitles," title cards inserted into the film to share key plot points or dialogue. When movies were shown in the theater, live musicians played piano and other instruments to enhance the emotional twists and turns of the story.

Journalist, screenwriter, and director **Frances Marion (1888–1973)** wrote over 323 scripts in a long career that started with silent films and moved into "talkies." Frances was well known for adapting books and stories into film scripts. During World War II, she traveled overseas to be a combat correspondent, writing about women's roles in the war effort.

Technology improved rapidly, and movies added length, sound, and color. Companies made stories in multiple genres, including horror, musicals, and drama. Longer films required more comprehensive scripts. The first example of a modern script was written for George Méliès's 1902 silent film, *A Trip to the Moon*. The script consisted of thirty lines that captured the setting and the action with phrases like "Wild Pursuit," "Splashing into the Open Sea," and "Take Prisoners!!"

Around the same time, filmmakers recruited comic artists to create animated films. In 1928, Walt Disney made *Steamboat Willie*, starring Mickey Mouse, one of the first animated cartoons with synchronized sound. At Disney Studios, the process of writing a script was a collaborative effort. For the movie *Snow White and the Seven Dwarfs*, a staff writer made notes about characters, scenes, and potential jokes. The company met to develop the storyline, and then the team created a storyboard.

When filmmaking moved to California, Hollywood studios became big business and employed screenwriters, directors, actors, designers, and more.

Producers organized all aspects of the production. The screenwriter, or "photo playwright," wrote the story and handed it off to the producer, who used the script to set a budget and ensure continuity in the film.

In the 1950s, the studio approach to movie making ended. The director was seen as the "author" of a movie because they brought together all aspects of the production. This meant that famous directors like Alfred Hitchcock were credited for a movie's success even when they did not write the script.

In the 1960s, writers began creating scripts "on spec." Any writer could write a screenplay and pitch it to a studio. Suddenly, screenwriters were important again and were given credit—and awards—for their work.

Today, screenwriters focus on creating a readable script with strong story elements: a marketable concept, a distinct theme, rich characters, and an engaging plot. Once a script is bought, the director creates a shooting script, adding locations, camera angles, and all other technical details. Better special effects make it possible for writers to see their wildest dreams captured on film.

Thanks to huge jumps in technology, anyone with a computer and a camera can now write, direct, produce, and distribute their own film. As Walt Disney said, "If you can dream it, you can do it."

Jordan Peele (1979–) is an actor, comedian, writer, and director who wrote sketch comedy for *Mad TV* and *Key and Peele* before turning to screenwriting. He wrote and directed the film *Get Out*, becoming the first Black American to win the Academy Award for Best Original Screenplay. He also wrote and hosted the new version of *The Twilight Zone*.

WRITE TO KNOW

So, you want to be a screenwriter? People write scripts for many kinds of productions, including:

- Video games
- Commercials
- Television shows
- Instructional videos
- Fiction podcasts
- Web series

WRITE NOW

What story could you tell in three minutes or less?

The Très Court International Film Festival limits its entries to films that are less than three minutes long, and the international film festival Filminute presents one-minute films. Develop a concept for a very short film. Write the script, including directions for shooting. Then gather your actors—and shoot!

Transgender filmmakers **Lana (1965–) and Lilly Wachowski (1967–)** wrote comic books before creating films like *The Matrix*. The sisters grew up reading comics and playing video games. Lilly said, "That's why I gravitated toward science fiction and fantasy. . . . It was all about creating worlds. I think it freed us up as filmmakers because we were able to imagine stuff at that time that you didn't necessarily see onscreen."

You have many years ahead of you to create the dreams that we can't even imagine dreaming.

—*Steven Spielberg*

Maria Merian

Naturalist and Scientific Illustrator,
1647–1717

Write to Wonder:
*The Metamorphosis
of the Insects of Surinam*

Have you ever noticed fruit flies swarming around brown bananas? Or found silverfish munching on the pages of your old books? How did these insects infest these common items?

In the 1600s, when Maria Merian was a little girl growing up in Frankfurt, Germany, people believed that insects grew from inanimate objects like meat, wool, and dung. Maria questioned this theory.

Maria's stepfather was an artist who painted ornamental flowers and other still-life subjects. She captured insects for him to paint. As she worked, Maria wondered where the insects came from and how they grew and changed. Maria investigated the life cycle of insects. At thirteen, she experimented with silkworms, watching every step of their journey from caterpillar to moth. She captured this cycle in detailed drawings.

When Maria grew up, she married one of her father's apprentices. At thirty-two, Maria published her first book, *The Wondrous Transformation of Caterpillars and Their Particular Nourishment from Flowers*, which included detailed drawings of the life cycle of more than fifty moths and butterflies. She was the first woman to publish about how caterpillars were transformed into butterflies.

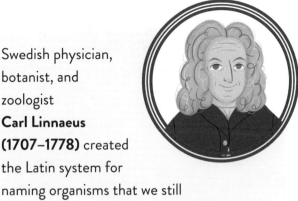

Swedish physician, botanist, and zoologist **Carl Linnaeus (1707–1778)** created the Latin system for naming organisms that we still use today. He relied on Maria Merian's insect discoveries in his book *Systema Naturae*, which classified animals and plants.

When she was thirty-eight, Maria left her husband. After living in a religious community, she moved to Amsterdam. She supported herself by selling her paintings. After researching, writing, and publishing a second volume about caterpillars, Maria wanted to know if the creatures in other parts of the world had the same life cycle as European caterpillars. Maria didn't have a sponsor like other Dutch naturalists, so she sold 255 of her paintings to finance a trip to Surinam in South America, where she could study a whole new world of insects.

In Surinam, the local residents ridiculed her for studying plants and insects. But her research proved her theory: even across the globe, insects also went through a cycle of transformation. Maria turned her research into the book *The Metamorphosis of the Insects of Surinam*, a collection of sixty life-size scenes in which she portrayed the life cycle of several new species of insects and plants. She dedicated the book to "all lovers and investigators of nature."

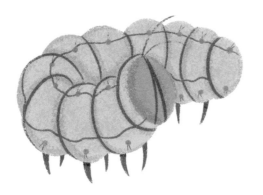

Maria's investigations helped change the way people thought about insects. They did not spontaneously emerge from dead things but grew from eggs. Each insect had its own cycle of growth. Her work influenced the way scientists studied and displayed their work, portraying insects inside their environment, with their host plants, instead of showing them in isolation.

WRITE TO KNOW

Maria Merian kept a research diary or field journal, in which she sketched detailed pictures of what she observed in nature. In a field journal, researchers record basic facts and note sensory details—what they see, hear, taste, touch, and smell. Here's what you might include in a field journal:

- Time, date, and location
- Guiding questions
- Jottings
- Description
- Analysis
- Reflection

From youth on I have been occupied with the investigation of insects.

—*Maria Merian*

Marie Curie (1867–1934) cataloged chemical elements and documented experiments in a lab notebook. Because she carried bottles of polonium and radium in her pocket, her scientific notebooks are literally radioactive.

WRITE NOW

Many scientific discoveries happened because people wondered about something, asked questions, and then observed the world around them. Choose a process to observe—like the colony of ants living in your backyard or the dried bean you're hoping will sprout into a plant—and keep a detailed record of it over a period of time. Use both writing and drawing.

Sor Juana Inés de la Cruz

Poet, Dramatist,
and Religious Writer, 1651–1695

Write to Defend:
"Reply to Sor Filotea"

Before Juana turned three, she tagged along to her sister's lessons and "felt the desire to learn to read burn within." She told the teacher her mother had arranged for lessons. She hadn't. Juana got them anyway. When she was six, Juana heard about the university in Mexico City and wanted in.

> *I began to pester my mother to death with constant and inopportune pleas to dress me as a boy and send me to Mexico City to the home of some of her relatives so that I could study and take courses at the university.*

Juana's family refused to send her to school. She secretly read her grandfather's books, teaching herself multiple languages and subjects. When she was eight, she wrote a one-act play for a contest and won a book.

In Juana's day, young women had two choices: marrying or entering the convent. Juana did not want to marry. Juana Ramírez de Asbaje took the name Sor ("Sister") Juana Inés de la Cruz when she became a cloistered nun, living separate from the world. At the convent, Sor Juana had a small room that held her books, musical instruments, scientific equipment, maps, and works of art. She taught at the convent school and worked as the convent's archivist and accountant. Between tasks, she wrote poetry, liturgical and public drama, and theology. Sor Juana believed God had called her to write, and this work was as important as physical labor.

Playwright and political activist **Olympia de Gorges (1748–1793)** called for gender equality when she wrote "The Declaration of the Rights of Women and the Female Citizen." During the French Revolution, she was arrested for writings that championed the citizen's right to vote. She was sentenced to death and was executed.

Maria, the Countess de Paredes, became Sor Juana's patron and helped her publish and promote her writing in both Europe and the Americas. Sor Juana had fans all over the world who commissioned work from her.

Sor Juana communicated with Maria and others through letters and visits in the convent parlor, where a screened wall separated the nuns from their visitors. At one conversation circle, a bishop heard Sor Juana critique a sermon. He asked her to send him her argument.

When I say something, poetry results.

—Sor Juana Inés de la Cruz

The bishop published Sor Juana's critique without her permission. Using the pseudonym Sister Filotea, he also released a letter scolding Sor Juana for having "wasted much time in the study of philosophers and poets." He suggested she read "the book of Jesus Christ" or risk spending eternity in hell.

Mary Wollstonecraft (1759–1797) was one of the first women to work independently as an author, translating texts and writing book reviews. She wrote "A Vindication of the Rights of Women," a feminist philosophy supporting a woman's right to an education.

Sor Juana wrote the "Reply to Sor Filotea" to defend herself and a woman's right to study theology, "the queen of the sciences." She showed that understanding the Bible required studying many disciplines, including law, architecture, and history. She wrote about how God created her hungry to learn and cited the accomplishments of women in ancient history and the Bible. Sor Juana used sarcasm to express her anger at the bishop for sharing her private thoughts with the public: "The second impossibility is to know how to thank you for such an excessive, unexpected favor, namely the publishing of my scribblings."

After Sor Juana sent this letter, she renewed her vows and sold most of her books, giving the money to the poor. She wrote very little after that. We don't know if she chose this path or if her superiors were punishing her. In 1695, she died while tending to the sisters during an outbreak of the plague.

Afterward, a poem was found in her study that reflected on the publication of her second book of poems. There was evidence that she was rebuilding her library. Perhaps Sor Juana had not given up writing.

Sor Juana's "Reply to Sor Filotea" was published after her death and became Mexico's first female manifesto. Sor Juana's writing and outspoken nature earned her the nicknames "the Tenth Muse" and "the Phoenix of Mexico."

WRITE TO KNOW

A manifesto is a published declaration of rights, objectives, intentions, views, or a plan of action. Manifestos often attack the status quo and announce a vision for a new future.

WRITE NOW

Sor Juana Inés de la Cruz told her story to defend women's rights. Write a manifesto defending rights that matter to you. Use your story and any other evidence that will help you make your argument.

WRITE TO CREATE

Sor Juana's image graced the 200-peso bank note for forty-one years. Create a bank note, or dollar bill, featuring the image of your favorite author or yourself.

Phillis Wheatley

Poet, 1753–1784

Write to Remember:
"On Being Brought
from Africa to America"

As a seven-year-old girl, Phillis Wheatley was kidnapped, forced from her home in Gambia, West Africa, and brought to Boston. She arrived ill, clutching an old, dirty carpet around herself. Susanna and John Wheatley purchased the "slender, frail female child" and named her Phillis after the ship she'd traveled on. She would suffer from asthma her entire life.

Enslaved by the Wheatleys, Phillis worked as their household servant. The family noticed her interest in words and taught her to read. Phillis studied astronomy, geography, and history. She read the Bible, Greek and Latin classics, and British literature. She also wrote poetry, publishing her first poem in the local paper at age thirteen.

In 1770, Phillis heard evangelical Methodist minister George Whitfield preach. He died

a week later, and Phillis wrote an elegy for him. Her poem was published with the funeral sermon and reprinted many times in both America and Great Britain. Suddenly, Phillis Wheatley was a famous poet.

In 1761, the preacher **Jupiter Hammon (1711–1806)** became the first Black American to publish a poem. He wrote the poem "An Address to Miss Phillis Wheatley" to encourage her faith.

A year later, Phillis had written enough poems to publish a book. Countess Selina Hastings, who had been a good friend of George Whitfield, financed *Poems on Various Subjects, Religious and Moral.*

In the summer of 1773, the Wheatleys' son Nathaniel took Phillis to London. She hoped to meet her sponsor and help see the book into print. During her stay, Phillis met with British leaders, abolitionists, and visiting dignitaries like Benjamin Franklin. But before she could meet the countess, Phillis was summoned back to nurse the ill Susanna Wheatley. Historians believe Phillis negotiated a deal with Nathaniel: she would return only if the family promised to grant her freedom.

A few months after Phillis returned to America, the Wheatleys freed Phillis. She later wrote:

> *. . . for in every human Breast, God has implanted a Principle, which we call Love of Freedom; it is impatient of Oppression, and pants for Deliverance; and by the Leave of our modern Egyptians I will assert, that the same Principle lives in us.*

By this time, the American Revolution had begun, and Phillis wrote several poems to celebrate America and its first president, George Washington. She sent him a poem, and he wrote back, praising her work. The two met in 1776 at his headquarters in Cambridge, Massachusetts.

Born in slavery, **George Moses Horton (1798–1867)** taught himself to read. In 1829, George released his first book of poems, *The Hope of Liberty*, and became the first Black man to publish a book in the South.

After Susanna and John Wheatley died, Phillis married John Peters, a free Black man. They lived in poverty and were often in debt. Phillis kept writing, publishing proposals for poetry books in 1779 and 1784. Later that year, she died, along with one of her children.

Phillis Wheatley was the first Black woman, the first female enslaved person, and the second woman to publish a book of poems in America. The style and content of her poetry demonstrate that Phillis had absorbed her classical education and Christian teachings. She wrote poems against slavery that influenced readers abroad and in America.

While an intrinsic ardor prompts to write,
The muses promise to assist my pen.

—*Phillis Wheatley*

By the time **Gwendolyn Brooks (1917–2000)** was sixteen, she'd published seventy-five poems. She wrote about the struggles of poor Black people in Chicago and used her writing to fight social and racial injustice.

WRITE TO KNOW

Writers remember loved ones by writing an obituary, a eulogy, or an elegy. An elegy can take many forms and use a variety of poetic elements. Phillis Wheatley loved the couplet, two lines of verse in the same meter or rhythm that rhyme. She also used these poetic elements:

ALLITERATION: when two or more words start with the same sound

ASSONANCE: when vowel sounds are repeated

CONSONANCE: when consonant sounds are repeated

WRITE NOW

Phillis Wheatley used the elegy form to suggest to readers that they needed to bury certain beliefs and practices, like being slave owners. What problem, trend, or movement do you think needs to end? Write an elegy for it.

Wang Zhenyi

Mathematician and Poet, 1768–1797

Write to Explain: "The Explanation of the Solar Eclipse"

When Wang Zhenyi lived, Chinese society expected men to fulfill the proverb "Tread ten thousand miles and read ten thousand books." Wang claimed this goal for herself, writing, "I once compared my ambition to a kind even / Stronger than a man's."

In those days, women had no legal rights and were educated for the sole purpose of managing the household. Fortunately, Wang Zhenyi was born into a bookish family. Her father wrote a four-volume collection called *Collection of Medical Prescriptions*. He taught his daughter medicine, geography, and math. She learned poetry from her grandmother and astronomy from her grandfather. Her grandfather possessed seventy-five bookshelves filled with reading material. When he died, the family traveled to Jiling, near the Great Wall, for the funeral. For the next five years, Wang studied the books from her grandfather's shelves. She befriended educated women from the area and learned equestrian skills, archery, and martial arts. She wrote this about the women:

Accompanying my elders, I traveled far to the extraordinary places of interest to expand my scope of knowledge. I also met the talented gentry ladies from all across the empire. Enjoying thousands of poems in the mornings and hundreds of works of art in the evenings, we filled up our bags and cases with exchanged writings.

Wang liked the book *Principles of Calculation* by Mei Wending (1633–1721), but it was written in aristocratic Chinese and most people couldn't read it. Wang rewrote it in simpler language and published it as *The Musts of Calculation*. She also developed an easier method for multiplying and dividing numbers and explained the process in her book *The Simple Principles of Calculation*. It wasn't an easy task. She declared in her writings, "There were times that I had to put down my pen and sigh. But I love the subject, I do not give up."

Wang knew that people believed eclipses were the work of an angry god, so she explained them. She created an exhibit in her garden pavilion using a round table as the earth, a crystal lamp as the sun, and a round mirror as the moon. She moved each item using astronomical principles and wrote up her findings in an article, "The Explanation of the Solar Eclipse." She helped readers

Caroline Lucretia Herschel (1750–1848) was just four feet tall, due to a childhood bout with typhus. Caroline discovered many comets in her lifetime and created a catalog of nebulae. She became the first paid female scientist and the first woman to receive a Gold Medal of the Royal Astronomical Society.

understand the true cause of eclipses, writing: "Actually, it's definitely because of the moon."

Wang Zhenyi wrote at least twelve books as well as academic articles and poems. Her writing argued for modern ideas, like the Western calendar—which wouldn't be used in China until 1912. Wang married at twenty-five, continuing to study and write. Just before she died at age twenty-nine, she gave her papers to a friend, asking that she preserve them. She gave herself

Hypatia (350–415) was one of the first female scholars, teaching math, astronomy, and philosophy in Alexandria, Egypt. She wrote commentaries on geometry and arithmetic and designed scientific instruments. She crafted an astrolabe, a portable astronomical calculator that helped people identify and analyze stars and planets and determine the latitude on land or sea. This became a scientific norm for many centuries. Hypatia was murdered by an angry crowd, and scholars still debate why.

The astronomer **Annie Jump Cannon (1863–1941)** developed a method for cataloging stars called the Harvard Classification Scheme, organizing stars based on their temperatures and spectral types. Annie, who was nearly deaf as a result of scarlet fever, discovered more than three hundred stars and five novas and classified more than 350,000 stars.

the literary name Jiangning Nushi, meaning "female intellectual from Jiangning."

WRITE NOW

Writers use poems, how-to books, comics, infographics, tweets, and more to explore difficult subjects. What topic do you wish you could explain to others? Write it up using the form that best suits your subject.

It's made to believe,
Women are the same as Men;
Are you not convinced,
Daughters can also be heroic?

—*Wang Zhenyi*

Sequoyah

Anthropologist, 1776–1843

Write to Save:
First Cherokee
Writing System

As a child, Sequoyah solved problems. His mother ran a trading post, and he managed the cattle and tended the garden. When he noticed that the cow's milk quickly turned sour on warm days, he built a small storage shed over the stream to keep it cool.

Born in the Cherokee town of Tuskegee, Sequoyah (also known as George Gist or Guess) was the son of a Virginia fur trader, who disappeared before he was born, and Wuteh, the Cherokee mother who raised him. The name Sequoyah comes from a Cherokee word that means "pig's foot," and historians think he was lame in one leg. No one knows how Sequoyah injured his leg—some think it was the result of an accident or an illness, like polio.

Sequoyah taught himself to be a silversmith and blacksmith. He made exquisite jewelry from melted coins and crafted metal tools that he decorated with silver. When his mother died, Sequoyah took over her trading post. He noticed that writing helped white people communicate with each other. Sequoyah became convinced that writing would help the Cherokee people record their wisdom, gain knowledge, and teach their children.

Sequoyah began developing a writing system for the Cherokee language. He tried creating a picture for each word or idea, but he knew no one would remember so many images. Finally, he created a symbol for each syllable. When he finished, Sequoyah's syllabary had eighty-six characters. Some came from a Latin book he had found. Other characters resembled Greek, Cyrillic, or Arabic letters.

Sequoyah taught the syllabary to his six-year-old daughter, Ahyokeh, and together they showed people how it worked. At a meeting with Cherokee elders, Sequoyah sent his daughter out of the room. He asked the leaders to say words, and wrote them down. When his daughter returned, she read each of the words. The Cherokee elders were excited that symbols could help them understand each other. Soon, they learned how to read and write too.

The new language spread quickly. The Cherokee wrote letters and kept accounts. In 1827, the tribe used their written language to write the Constitution of the Cherokee Nation. In 1828, the tribe launched the *Cherokee Phoenix*, the first national bilingual newspaper. Sequoyah's syllabary made it possible for the tribe to preserve their history, culture, and spiritual beliefs.

King Sejong (1397–1450) wanted the Korean people to be able to write down their ideas and stories in their own language. So he hired scholars to create a phonetic writing system, which made it possible for anyone who spoke Korean to learn how to read and write.

WRITE TO KNOW

Whether you publish your newspaper in print or online, it might contain:

- Feature articles
- News articles (local, national, international)
- Editorials
- Letters to the editor
- Political cartoons
- Special sections (business, finance, news, sports, lifestyle, entertainment, food, arts, religion, travel, society, comic strips, puzzles, and more)
- Reviews (books, movies, concerts, restaurants, and more)

- Calendar of events
- Notices (births, engagements, marriages, deaths, and more)
- Advertisements
- Photographs
- Photo essays

WRITE NOW

Thanks to the internet, people can create and publish their own online newspapers, magazines, and blogs. If you were to create a newspaper for your family or classroom, what would you include? Design and name your newspaper. Develop the first issue—either on paper or online.

The Vietnamese farmer and basket weaver **Shong Lue Yang (1929–1971)** had no formal education. Through a series of spiritual visions, he invented the Pahawh script, a syllabary for writing the Hmong and Khmu language. He was feared by the communist government and assassinated in 1971. The Hmong people have honored him with the title "Mother of Writing."

When a talk is made and put down, it is good to look at it afterward.

—*Sequoyah*

Write to Declare:
The United States Declaration of Independence

How do you break up with a king? If you're a fledgling collection of colonies hoping to become a new country, you write a declaration of independence.

During the Seven Years' War (1756–1763, sometimes called the French and Indian War), France, Great Britain, and Spain battled over control of the American colonies. In 1763, the Treaty of Paris gave Britain control of all of the colonies. But the war left Great Britain with debt. To raise money, they taxed the colonies on goods like tea, beer, and salt. When people rebelled, the British passed a series of acts that would help them regain control over the colonists.

The liberty of speaking and writing guards our other liberties.

—Thomas Jefferson

It didn't work. In September 1774, representatives from each colony met in Philadelphia for the First Continental Congress. They wrote a Declaration of Rights, listing their grievances to the king and saying that if he didn't stop the intolerable acts, they would boycott British goods.

Tensions grew. In 1775, shots were fired between British troops and the colonial militia. The "shot heard round the world" ignited the Revolutionary War.

When **Thomas Jefferson (1743–1826)** wrote the Declaration of Independence, he didn't set out to be original. Instead, he hoped to capture the beliefs of those who supported the American Revolution. He borrowed ideas and words from the philosopher John Locke, his own draft of the preamble to the Virginia Constitution, and Virginia's Declaration of Rights. The Congress made eighty-six changes to his draft, which irked Thomas. Years later, he'd send copies of his original draft to colleagues.

In the summer of 1776 at the Second Continental Congress, Virginian Richard Henry Lee proposed the Lee Resolution: that the colonies declare independence from Britain. Congress nominated a committee to write the declaration, and the committee debated who should compose the document. Thomas Jefferson wanted John Adams to write it. But Adams refused, later recounting his reasons in a letter:

Reason first, you are a Virginian, and a Virginian ought to appear at the head of this business. Reason second, I am obnoxious, suspected, and unpopular. You are very much otherwise. Reason third, you can write ten times better than I can.

Over the next seventeen days, in between meetings of the Congress, Thomas Jefferson wrote multiple drafts of the Declaration of Independence hunched over a desk in a room at a local boarding house. Although he was an enslaver, Jefferson included a passage that attacked Great Britain's support of slavery. But the Congress didn't think the southern colonies would pass the draft if it denounced slavery, so they removed that clause.

On July 2, the Second Continental Congress adopted the Lee Resolution, declaring that the thirteen colonies were free and independent states, separate from Great Britain, and would be known as the United States of America. Congress approved the final draft of the Declaration of Independence on July 4, 1776. The United States was free.

WRITE TO KNOW

By the end of 1776, the Declaration of Independence traveled around the world, and many people read translated versions of it. The document inspired other revolutionary leaders around the world to declare independence.

- "The Declaration of the Rights of Man and the Citizen" was created and drafted by the Abbé Sieyès and

Benjamin Franklin (1706–1790) didn't graduate from school, yet he invented the lightning rod, made important discoveries about electricity, owned several newspapers, and founded the University of Pennsylvania. He ran a newspaper, and under pseudonyms, he wrote political cartoons and founded *Poor Richard's Almanack*. In his autobiography, Benjamin published the daily schedule he kept to get so much done. He began each day by asking, "What good shall I do this day?"

the Marquis de Lafayette in France, in consultation with Thomas Jefferson, and adopted on August 26, 1789.

- The playwright and political activist Olympia de Gorges (1748–1793) called for gender equality in "The Declaration of the Rights of Women and the Female Citizen."
- At the Seneca Falls (New York) Convention, the first women's rights convention organized by women, the principal author, Elizabeth Cady Stanton, modeled the "Declaration of Sentiments" on the Declaration of Independence.
- More than half of the countries that are part of the United Nations now have a document similar to the Declaration of Independence.

George Mason (1725–1792) refused to sign the Declaration of Independence even though his writing inspired some of the most memorable lines. George had written Virginia's Declaration of Rights, and Thomas Jefferson drew on that work for lines like "We hold these truths to be self-evident, that all men are created equal." George Mason wanted the Declaration to end slavery and provide a bill of rights. When James Madison later wrote the Bill of Rights, he used the work of both George Mason and Thomas Jefferson.

WRITE NOW

What do you need to declare your independence from? Write a document declaring your freedom!

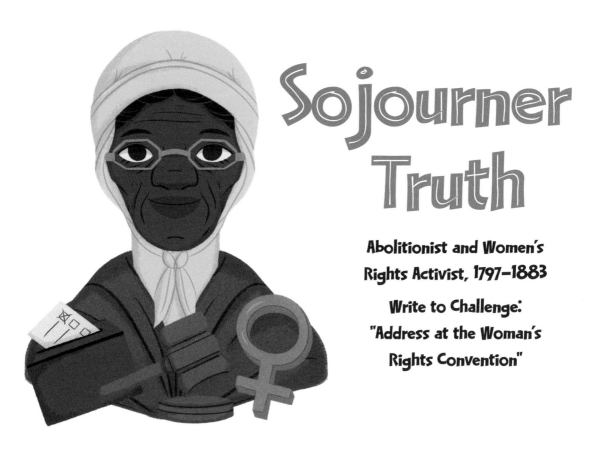

Sojourner Truth

**Abolitionist and Women's
Rights Activist, 1797–1883**

Write to Challenge:
**"Address at the Woman's
Rights Convention"**

Even though Sojourner Truth could not read or write, she made her living as an author, speaker, and activist.

Born enslaved in New York state and named Isabella Baumfree, Sojourner spoke only Dutch until she was eleven. When she was thirty and the mother of five children, her enslaver promised to release her. After he broke that promise, she ran away with her youngest child, Sophie. She later sued to rescue her five-year-old son, Peter, from slavery in Alabama and won the case.

Truth is powerful and it prevails.

—Sojourner Truth

In 1843, Isabella changed her name to Sojourner Truth and began traveling around the country, preaching against slavery at camp meetings and other events. She had a powerful voice and broke into song during every speech. Sojourner sold *cartes de visite* souvenirs, photographs mounted on cards, to fund her speaking tours. She added this quote to each photo: "I sell the shadow to support the substance."

Harriet Ann Jacobs (1831–1897) wrote *Incidents in the Life of a Slave Girl* to teach white women in the North how enslavers abused enslaved persons in multiple ways. After publishing her book, Harriet founded a school for Black people.

In the 1840s, when slave narratives became popular, Sojourner dictated her story to a friend. Sojourner published *Narrative of Sojourner Truth: A Northern Slave* (1850) by herself, paying for it from the proceeds of the book. Later, she acquired the printing plates and issued several revised editions of the book.

In 1851, Sojourner Truth launched a speaking tour to sell her book. She appeared at the Women's Rights Convention in Akron, Ohio, when it was illegal for escaped enslaved persons to enter or settle in the state. No wonder Sojourner was the only Black person in the room when she gave her famous speech.

During her talk, Sojourner spoke against slavery and for women's rights. Men considered women the weaker sex and dependent on men, believing they did not need their own rights. Sojourner argued: "I have as much muscle as any man, and can do as much work as any man." She knocked down the idea that because Jesus was a man, women should not have a role in public life. Sojourner reminded hearers how Jesus came into the world: "Through God who created him and woman who bore him. Man, where is your part?" Sojourner took the idea that women couldn't vote because they were the source of sin and turned it upside down:

> *I have heard the bible and have learned that Eve caused man to sin. Well if woman upset the world, do give her a chance to set it right side up again.*

Twelve years after the speech, the conference organizer published an account of Sojourner's speech that gave her a Southern dialect and added the refrain "Ain't I a Woman?" Sojourner included the version in a later edition of her *Narrative*, but historians do not believe she actually said those words.

Sojourner's speech on women's rights was just one highlight of her long career as a speaker, activist, and author. On an 1865 trip to Washington, DC, Sojourner Truth waged a one-woman campaign against segregation on the streetcars. She'd ride on the whites-only horse-drawn cars, refusing to move. A conductor tried to toss Sojourner off the streetcar and dislocated her arm. Sojourner sued the District of Columbia and won. The conductor lost his job, and the company had to enforce DC's desegregation law.

Professor and feminist **bell hooks (1952–)** was inspired by Sojourner Truth's speech to write her book *Ain't I a Woman: Black Women and Feminism* (1981). Hooks explores the effect of racism and sexism on Black women during slavery and afterward. She wrote, "Life-transforming ideas have always come to me through books."

After the Civil War, Sojourner helped freed men and women find jobs. She advocated for their civil rights. And Sojourner fought for voting rights for both Black and white women. From the late 1850s on, Sojourner was a popular enough speaker to draw a crowd on her own. In the preface to her book, Sojourner wrote: "I am a self-made woman." And indeed she was.

Eliza Suggs (1876–1908) wrote the book *Shadow and Sunshine*, which tells the stories of how her parents experienced and escaped slavery. Eliza suffered from brittle-bone disease.

WRITE NOW

Write your own speech that protests the common ideas of who you should be or how you should act.

Louis Braille

Inventor and Educator, 1809–1852

Write to Read: *Method of Writing Words, Music, and Plain Songs by Means of Dots, for Use by the Blind and Arranged for Them*

Growing up in a small French town, Louis Braille loved watching his father make harnesses in his workshop. When he was three, Louis grabbed an awl and tried to punch a hole in a piece of leather. But as he pressed down, the tool slipped and stabbed him in the eye.

The town doctor patched Louis's eye and sent him to a surgeon in Paris. The surgeon could not save his eye. The wound became infected and spread to the other eye. Louis was completely blind by the time he was five. This experience confused him, and he asked his parents, "Why is it always dark?"

> We must be treated as equals—and communication is the way this can be brought about.
>
> —*Louis Braille*

Louis's parents had never known a blind person before. But they cherished the youngest of their four children and did what they could to help him. Louis's father carved a cane for him, teaching him to walk the country paths. His parents sent him to the country school, where the students recited literature. Louis learned quickly.

Louis's parents knew that he needed to learn how to read and write to support himself. When he was ten, they arranged for him to enter the Royal Institute for Blind Youth in Paris. The school's founder had developed a system to teach the students to read. He designed and made books with raised letters that students could touch to understand. To write home, Louis traced leather letters to compose his messages.

When Louis was a teenager, Captain Charles Barbier of the French Army came to the school and demonstrated "night writing." The captain had devised a code of raised dots and dashes that allowed soldiers to communicate with each other on the battlefield.

Louis was captivated by night writing, but thought it was too complicated. Louis simplified the code, creating a system that allowed blind people to read and write. Because he was a gifted musician, playing both organ and cello, Louis also developed a method for musical notation.

When the writer and cartoonist **James Thurber (1894–1961)** was seven, his brother shot him in the eye with an arrow during a game of William Tell. After losing sight in that eye, he spent more time inside and developed his creativity. He said, "The kingdom of the partly blind is a little like Oz, a little like Wonderland. . . . Anything you can think of, and a lot you would never think of, can happen there."

In 1829, he published a book on the process, *Method of Writing Words, Music, and Plain Songs by Means of Dots, for Use by the Blind and Arranged for Them.*

The school recognized Louis's abilities as a student and musician. They hired him first as a teacher's aide and then as a full professor, teaching geometry, algebra, and history. Louis Braille wrote many books about education and his system of writing, now called Braille in honor of him.

Poet and short story writer **Jorge Luis Borges (1899–1986)** was born sighted and went blind over time due to a hereditary eye disorder. He never learned Braille and depended on his mother to be his personal secretary. Jorge achieved academic success as the director of the National Public Library and a professor of English literature at the University of Buenos Aires, Argentina. He saw his blindness as a gift: "A writer . . . must believe that whatever happens to him is an instrument, everything has been given for an end."

Louis developed tuberculosis when he was twenty-six years old. When he was forty, he moved back to his hometown due to poor health. When Louis died at age forty-three, his school was still not teaching Braille. Two years later, largely as a result of pressure from the students, the Royal Institute adopted the Braille method. By 1882, Braille was used in most places in Europe, and by 1916 it was used by schools in the United States. In 1932, English-speaking countries approved a uniform Braille code.

World Braille Day is celebrated every year on Louis Braille's birthday, January 4. All over the world, people honor the blind teenager whose curiosity and persistence led him to develop a system that allows millions of people to read, write, and live independent lives.

WRITE NOW

People are always inventing new ways of communicating. Do you think Louis Braille could have imagined texting? Write a text message poem—using textspeak or regular language.

Belo Cipriani (1980–) was blinded in a brutal attack and wrote about it in his memoir, *Blind*. Belo works as a disability advocate and activist, specializing in helping people in the LGBTQIA+ community. He founded Oleb Books to publish the work of writers with disabilities.

WRITE TO CREATE

Charles Barbier's night-writing system was connected to the Polybius square, invented by the ancient Greeks to send coded messages. Write a message to a friend in code. Can they figure it out?

Charles Darwin

Naturalist, 1809–1882

Write to Experiment: *On the Origin of the Species by Means of Natural Selection, or, The Preservation of Favored Races in the Struggle for Life*

At boarding school, nine-year-old Charles Darwin loathed memorizing and often skipped class. He hunted bugs and made laughing gas, returning to school just before curfew.

Charles's father wanted him to be a doctor, but Charles felt faint at the sight of blood. When Charles dropped out of medical school, his father said, "You care for nothing but shooting, dogs, and rat-catching, and you will be a disgrace to yourself and all your family."

Charles moved to Cambridge University, where he took up the popular hobby of the day—collecting beetles—and began his lifelong study of the natural world.

Shortly after graduating, Charles worked as a captain's companion on an exploration journey to South America. Despite persistent seasickness, he traveled around the world for five years. Charles gathered more than 1,500 specimens, recorded 1,383 pages of notes on geology, and wrote 368 pages on

> ## I am a complete millionaire in odd and curious little facts.
>
> *—Charles Darwin*

plants and animals. He also composed a 770-page diary, which he revised and published. This data fueled his writing for the rest of his life.

Charles tracked his scientific ideas in small notebooks, each labeled with a letter. He recorded his first ideas about evolution in his B notebook—but didn't share this with the world for twenty years. Historians call this Darwin's Delay. Some think Charles procrastinated because he worried that readers would be upset that his theory contradicted the Bible.

Charles was also busy with his wife and ten children. He suffered from a debilitating illness that included stomach pain, vomiting, gas, chronic fatigue, and episodes of fear and sadness. Plus, he wanted more proof and conducted many research projects, enlisting his children's help.

Charles wrote the first draft of his theory in 1842. He proposed that diverse life forms can be traced back to a few common ancestors. Surviving species adapt to a changing environment, often by developing

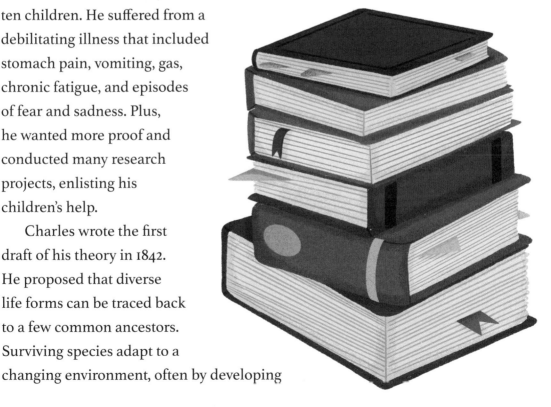

new traits. Two years later, Charles expanded the theory to a 230-page book and shelved it.

In 1858, Alfred Russel Wallace, a self-educated naturalist, sent his paper on evolution to Charles, requesting help publishing it. Charles worried that Alfred would get credit for the idea he'd been working on for years.

His friends presented the naturalist's paper and Charles's work to a scientific-society meeting, giving detailed proof of his research history. Charles couldn't be there—he was attending his youngest son's funeral. Afterward, the president of the society wrote that none of the day's papers included revolutionary discoveries.

Charles quickly revised his book for publication. Determined to make his ideas accessible to the average person, he used pigeons and dogs as examples. Charles also shared loads of data to prove his theory.

On the Origin of the Species was published on November 24, 1859—and the date has become known as the birthday of modern biology. Charles Darwin's theory about evolution created a paradigm shift: humans, the earth, and the universe are not stable but constantly changing. This theory would transform biology, psychology, medicine, agriculture, and more. The library at Charles's own alma mater, Trinity College, Cambridge, immediately banned his book. In 2019, *On the Origin of the Species* was named the most influential banned book of all time.

Darwin discovered fossils in South America, spurring his ideas about evolution. The artist **Leonardo da Vinci (1452–1519)** studied rocks and discovered that fossils were the remains of living beings. He recorded his ideas in notebooks and protected them by using mirror writing.

The big green book was 502 pages long and would go through six editions in Charles Darwin's lifetime. It wasn't until the fifth edition that Charles used the phrase "survival of the fittest." And for the record, Charles Darwin never said that people were descended from monkeys.

WRITE TO KNOW

The scientific method gives scientists a process for proving a theory by collecting evidence. Here are the steps:

1. Make an observation.
2. Ask a question.
3. Form a hypothesis.
4. Test the hypothesis with an experiment.
5. Analyze evidence and draw conclusions.
6. Accept or reject the hypothesis and communicate results.

WRITE NOW

What theories would you like to explore? Using the scientific method, create a hypothesis and test it! Write a report that encourages readers to adopt your discoveries.

Ada Lovelace

Algorithm Writer, 1815–1852

Write to Visualize: "Sketch of the Analytical Engine Invented by Charles Babbage, Esq., with Notes by the Translator: Ada Lovelace"

Ada Lovelace dreamed of soaring through the air and tried to invent a flying machine. She wrote:

> *I have got a scheme to make a thing in the form of a horse with a steam engine in the inside so contrived as to move an immense pair of wings, fixed on the outside of the horse, in such a manner as to carry it up into the air while a person sits on its back.*

Twelve-year-old Ada studied the anatomy of birds. She investigated materials like feathers, paper, and silk, hoping they might mimic wings. She designed a winged apparatus and included it in her illustrated guide, *Flyology*.

When Ada confessed her dream to her mother, she chastised Ada for neglecting her math studies. Ada Lovelace was the daughter of the poet

Lord Byron, who was a rising social star known for his brilliant poetry, and Anne Isabella Milbanke, whom Byron called the princess of parallelograms. Lady Byron designed an educational program for Ada built around history, geography, languages, chemistry, math, music, and sewing. Because of her classical education, Ada developed an extraordinary ability to speak poetically about science and math.

Grace Hopper (1906–1992) created a programming tool that used words instead of numbers, called COBOL (Common Business Orientated Language). When a moth got stuck in her computer, she coined the terms *bug* and *debugging*.

When she was seventeen, Ada Lovelace met Charles Babbage, a mathematician and mechanical engineer. He showed her his "Difference Machine," which could make calculations by turning a handle. Ada was intrigued, and the two began corresponding.

In a letter, Ada asked, "What is imagination?" She mused that it was twofold, the combining faculty and the discovering faculty. Ada believed that those who could combine science and imagination could soar further into new territories. And that's just what she did.

When her friend Charles Babbage designed an analytical machine and presented it at a conference in Italy, a colleague wrote about it. Knowing

If you can't give me poetry, can't you give me "poetical science"?

—*Ada Lovelace*

In 1613, a writer used the term *computer* to refer to a mathematician. In the late nineteenth century, the term *computer* referred to people—mostly women—who performed complex calculations for scientists. The computer we know today got its name because it took the jobs of human "computers."

Ada's knack for explaining complex concepts, Charles suggested she translate the article and add her own notes. Ada's writing ended up being three times the length of the original article.

Ada Lovelace described how the analytic machine could be programmed using pierced cards. She wrote, "The Analytical Engine weaves algebraical patterns just as the Jacquard-loom weaves flowers and leaves."

But she didn't stop there: Ada created a detailed computer program—the first computer code. She predicted that these kinds of codes would someday enable machines to create music and art and possibly think on their own.

Ada Lovelace was also one of the first people to visualize and articulate an idea called universal computation, that a single piece of hardware can be programmed to do any sort of computation. She wrote this about the machine: "It can do whatever we know how to order it to

Next time you ask your phone for directions, thank **Gladys Mae West (1930–)**. Gladys programmed a computer to calculate the shape of the earth. Her work became the foundation for the Global Positioning System (GPS).

perform." Ada inspired generations of thinkers to imagine new ways computers can function.

WRITE NOW

Do you dream of doing something impossible? Write a how-to guide and illustrate it.

WRITE TO CREATE

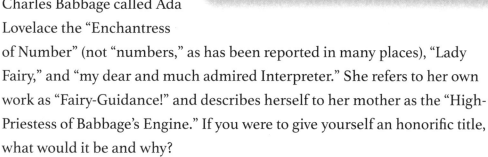

During World War II, **Elizabeth Holberton (1917–2001)** calculated missile trajectories. Afterward, the United States Army recruited her to be a programmer for its electronic digital computer (ENIAC) program. She used a deck of playing cards to write the first generative programming system (Sort/Merge).

Charles Babbage called Ada Lovelace the "Enchantress of Number" (not "numbers," as has been reported in many places), "Lady Fairy," and "my dear and much admired Interpreter." She refers to her own work as "Fairy-Guidance!" and describes herself to her mother as the "High-Priestess of Babbage's Engine." If you were to give yourself an honorific title, what would it be and why?

Frederick Douglass

Abolitionist and Orator, 1818–1895

Write to Free: *Narrative of a Life of Frederick Douglass, an American Slave, Written by Himself*

When he was eight, Frederick discovered that reading and writing could help set him free from slavery.

Frederick had just been sent to work at the home of Hugh and Sophia Auld. He saw Sophia reading the Bible and asked her to teach him to read. Her husband found out and forbade more lessons, saying that reading would make Frederick unfit for slavery. Frederick later wrote, "From that moment, I understood the pathway from slavery to freedom."

During errands for the family, Frederick would bet white street urchins that he could write better than they could. Frederick watched as they scratched words into dirt:

> *During this time, my copy-book was the board fence, brick wall, and pavement; my pen and ink was a lump of chalk. With these, I learned mainly how to write.*

After learning to read, Frederick helped teach reading to a group of enslaved persons. Hugh Auld caught him, showing up with a group of men carrying sticks. Frederick was sent to an enslaver who beat the sixteen-year-old so regularly, his wounds didn't have time to heal. After almost a year, Frederick fought back. He called this moment the turning point in his life, inspiring his determination to be free.

Known as Dave the Potter, **David Drake (1801–1870s)** was an enslaved person who crafted beautiful pots and inscribed them with his name and his poetry. These short verses preserved Dave the Potter's unique view of life as an enslaved person.

The enslaver sent Frederick back to the Aulds, where he worked on a ship. He borrowed the papers of a free Black sailor who looked nothing like him. Frederick hopped on a train. Twenty-four hours later, after taking two trains and a ferry ride, being questioned by a conductor, and avoiding several people he knew, Frederick landed in New York City. But he wasn't safe—slave catchers roamed the city.

A few days later, Frederick married Anna, a free woman he'd met when he was nineteen. They moved to Massachusetts, where he changed his last name to Douglass to evade capture. He did odd jobs until he discovered the anti-slavery newspaper *The Liberator* and decided to speak against slavery.

In my imagination, I already saw myself wielding my pen as well as my voice in the great work of renovating the public mind.

—*Frederick Douglass*

THE NORTH STAR.

The Massachusetts Anti-Slavery Society hired Frederick as a full-time speaker. He traveled with the "Hundred Conventions" project, a six-month tour through the United States. Frederick endured physical attacks from people against ending slavery, including one that broke his hand.

In 1845, Frederick wrote his autobiography, *The Narrative of a Life of an American Slave*. He sold five thousand copies of his book in the first four months, and it was translated into German and French. Because Frederick named real people and places in his book, he worried his former enslavers might pursue and capture him. When he traveled to Ireland and England to speak, his British supporters purchased his freedom. Frederick could finally live and travel without fear.

Frederick Douglass spent the rest of his life writing and fighting for freedom and equal rights for Black people. He started *The North Star*, a paper for Black people with the motto "Right is of no sex. Truth is of no color." Frederick opened his house as a stop on the Underground Railroad. During the Civil War, he fought for the rights of Black men to serve their country as soldiers and receive equal pay. Frederick also advocated for the integration of schools in Rochester, New York— and won.

Paul Laurence Dunbar (1872–1906) wrote his first poem at six and published a dozen books of poetry, as well as novels and short stories.

Later in life, Frederick moved to Washington, DC. He served several posts in the local and national government. He wrote two more volumes in his autobiography, *My Bondage and My Freedom* and *The Life and Times of Frederick Douglass*. Frederick spoke up for freedom until the very last day of his life.

WRITE TO KNOW

Frederick Douglass used figurative language in his memoir, *Narrative of a Life of Frederick Douglass*.

METAPHOR: Links two unlike items to illustrate. Frederick gave bread to street urchins in trade for the "bread of knowledge."

SIMILE: Uses *like* or *as* to compare. Frederick wrote about landing on free soil, "I felt like one who had escaped a den of hungry lions."

WRITE NOW

Write a prose poem about a significant event in your life, using figurative language.

Write to Abolish:
The Reconstruction Amendments

On September 17, 1862, as the morning fog lifted over a Maryland cornfield near Antietam Creek, the Union and Confederate troops engaged in the US Civil War lined up for battle. They were fighting over slavery. By the end of the day, more than 23,000 men would be injured or dead. The Union claimed victory in the Battle of Antietam, the bloodiest battle of the war.

President Abraham Lincoln knew it would take more than winning battles to abolish slavery. Just days later, he issued the Emancipation Proclamation, declaring that all enslaved persons in rebel states should be "forever free." The document focused the Civil War on the fight for freedom.

Although the president had spoken powerful words, his proclamation did not guarantee the freedom of enslaved persons. The United States needed to amend its constitution.

Beginning in December 1863, several senators and representatives presented amendments to end slavery. Two leaders wrote an amendment that began, "All persons are equal before the law, so that no person can hold another as a slave." The head of the Senate Judiciary Committee ignored this more expansive wording and merged other proposals to present the final draft of the amendment:

Neither slavery nor involuntary servitude, except as a punishment for crime whereof the party shall have been duly convicted, shall exist within the United States, or any place subject to their jurisdiction.

In April, the Senate passed the Thirteenth Amendment, but it failed in the House of Representatives. President Abraham Lincoln worried the Emancipation Proclamation might be reversed after the war. He invited individual members of Congress to his office to persuade them to pass the amendment. On January 31, 1865, the House approved the amendment by a narrow margin. Some members of Congress wept. In the gallery, free Black people cheered.

President Lincoln was assassinated in April. Eight months later, the Thirteenth Amendment became law.

Southern leaders wrote new state constitutions and passed "Black codes" to limit the rights of the newly

The preacher and abolitionist **Henry Highland Garnet (1815–1882)** became the first Black American to speak to Congress when he delivered his speech, "Let the Monster Perish," on February 12, 1865, to honor the Senate's adoption of the Thirteenth Amendment.

Booker T. Washington (1856–1915) was born into slavery. After working in salt furnaces and coal mines, he pursued his own education. At twenty-five, he became the head of the Tuskegee Normal and Industrial Institute and built it into Tuskegee University. He wrote fourteen books, including his autobiography, *Up from Slavery*. He was just nine years old when Abraham Lincoln issued the Emancipation Proclamation. Booker wrote:

> *Some man . . . made a little speech and then read a rather long paper—the Emancipation Proclamation, I think. After the reading we were told that we were all free, and could go when and where we pleased. My mother, who was standing by my side, leaned over and kissed her children, while tears of joy ran down her cheeks. She explained to us what it all meant, that this was the day for which she had been so long praying, but fearing that she would never live to see.*

freed Black Americans. In many states, Black people were not allowed to vote, learn to read and write, assemble freely, or choose their occupation.

To fight against the Black codes, Congress wrote and passed the Fourteenth and Fifteenth Amendments. The leaders wanted to ensure that Black Americans had equal rights and protections under the law. These three amendments are called the Reconstruction or Civil War Amendments.

The Civil War had ended. The leaders of the United States had successfully abolished slavery. But Black Americans were not free to exercise their unalienable rights of "Life, Liberty, and the pursuit of Happiness."

Verily, the work does not end with the abolition of slavery, but only begins.

—*Frederick Douglass*

Some leaders worried that because the Thirteenth Amendment included involuntary servitude as punishment for a crime, it allowed slavery to continue in another form. Prisons practiced "convict leasing," renting inmates out for day labor. Today, Black Americans are almost six times more likely to be imprisoned than white people. Because of this disparity, people are protesting the exception clause in the Thirteenth Amendment and working to get it removed.

In this and many other ways, Black Americans continue to fight for their civil rights, for an America where Black lives matter and where all people are treated equally under the law.

WRITE TO KNOW

When the delegates met in Philadelphia to draft the US Constitution, they knew that the country and its laws would need to change over time. So they wrote Article V, providing a process to amend the constitution. Since then, Congress has discussed thousands of amendments, rejected six, and approved twenty-seven.

WRITE NOW

Amendments allow governments, institutions, and other organizations to change their mind about what they believe or how they will function. What rules govern your life in your community, school, or family? How could an amendment bring a welcome change? Develop an amendment.

Florence Nightingale

Statistician and Founder of Nursing, 1820–1910

Write to Cure: Notes on Nursing: What It Is and What It Is Not

Six-year-old Florence Nightingale made a chart, recording her prayers and the dates she expected an answer. The results revealed that her prayers had been ignored. Florence wondered if God preferred action.

By the time she was a teenager, Florence was caring for family and neighbors, recording their ailments in a journal. Florence experienced a call from God to help poor and sick people. She took a course in nursing and became superintendent at a hospital.

The British government asked Florence to help the more than 18,000 soldiers injured in the Crimean War. When Florence and thirty-eight nurses arrived at the British base hospital in Turkey, they found the facility infested with rats, roaches, and lice. Injured men lined the hallways and curled up on the floor, many wrapped in filthy clothing and bed linens. The hospital sat on top of a cesspool, which contaminated the hospital's water supply.

> ## A thousand thanks for your bottle of ink. What should be without pens, ink and paper?
>
> —*Florence Nightingale*

Florence instructed nurses to bathe the patients and put them in fresh dressing gowns. Medical staff treated each patient with clean cloths. Florence worked with the staff to clean up the kitchens and provide healthier food. She got the British government to send a team to flush out the sewers. Florence made rounds each night, prompting the men to nickname her "the Lady with the Lamp." The death rate plummeted.

Florence kept meticulous records and wrote a detailed report about her work. She introduced a modified version of the pie chart—a coxcomb, or rose, chart—that helped readers understand that ten times more soldiers died from disease than from injuries. As a result, Florence became the first woman admitted to the Royal Statistical Society.

When she returned from the war, Florence established St. Thomas' Hospital and the Nightingale Training School for Nurses, the first official nurse training program. During the American Civil War, the United States government consulted her about how to run a field hospital.

Hildegard of Bingen (1098–1179) was a nun who wrote songs, poems, books, and two medical textbooks. In *Physica*, she documented how plants, stones, and animals can heal people from common ailments.

Although she never traveled to India, Florence performed a complicated statistical study of the country's sanitation system and helped improve both its sanitation and health care.

But Florence was not well. In Turkey, she'd come down with an illness that caused lifelong arthritis of the spine. She was bedridden off and on and suffered from depression.

In her lifetime, Florence Nightingale wrote more than two hundred books, pamphlets, and articles, as well as 19,000 letters. Her book *Notes on Nursing: What It Is and What It Is Not* was the first primer on nursing care. Much of her writing sparked worldwide health care reform.

WRITE TO KNOW

Did you catch a cold because of chilly air or a virus? Could you trace the cause and prevent getting sick in the future? A cause-and-effect diagram helps you identify a problem, analyze its causes, and explore possible solutions. You might discover that your problem has many causes, one effect; one cause, many effects; or a chain of causes and effects. Here's what a cause-and-effect diagram does:

- Describes a challenge and its characteristics
- Identifies major factors and potential causes
- Demonstrates how causes interact with each other
- Shows where there is a lack of information

Rebecca Lee Crumpler (1831–1895) was the first Black female physician in the United States. Passionate about helping women and children, she wrote *A Book of Medical Discourses in Two Parts* to promote their healthy care.

- Helps researchers examine a situation
- Discovers the root problem
- Finds a solution

WRITE NOW

Are you superstitious? Do you believe that Friday the 13th brings bad luck? Or that if a black cat crosses your path, you might be in for trouble? And don't even think about stepping on a crack! Choose a superstition and write a cause-and-effect diagram or document.

WRITE TO CREATE

Florence Nightingale used a coxcomb, or rose, chart to explain her discoveries. Today artists, scientists, and data journalists use visual storytelling to inform and inspire people. How might you use a chart, photos, or an infographic? Make one!

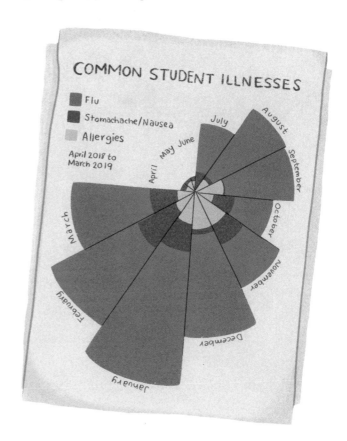

COMMON STUDENT ILLNESSES

- Flu
- Stomachache/Nausea
- Allergies

April 2018 to March 2019

January, February, March, April, May, June, July, August, September, October, November, December

Ida B. Wells

Investigative Journalist and Activist,
1862–1931

Write to Investigate:
Southern Horrors

When Ida Wells was sixteen, her parents and baby brother died of yellow fever. Determined to keep her remaining seven siblings together, she took a teaching job.

Ida commuted to her school by train. One day, she purchased a first-class ticket and sat in the Ladies' Coach. The conductor told her to move to the smoking car, with the other Black people. She refused. When the conductor tried to forcibly remove her, she bit his hand. He and his helpers tossed her off the train. They had torn her clothes and bruised her body, but Ida wasn't done fighting. She sued the railroad.

The people must know before they can act, and there is no educator to compare with the press.

—*Ida B. Wells*

The sociologist and historian **W. E. B. Du Bois (1868–1963)** cofounded the National Association for the Advancement of Colored People with Ida B. Wells. He published the foundational text *The Negro* (1915), a history of Black people in the United States.

To make extra money, Ida wrote and published stories in multiple newspapers. Readers loved her articles about politics, religion, and the problems she encountered as a teacher. Ida became so popular, her colleagues gave her the moniker "Princess of the Press."

The editor of a Memphis newspaper, *Memphis Free Speech and Headlight*, invited Ida to write for them. She agreed, as long as she could be part owner. Ida took over as editor and used her platform to speak against inequality, writing an article criticizing the state of schools for Black children. She was fired from her teaching job.

Ida needed to increase her income from writing. She printed the newspaper on pink paper to sell more copies. It worked—people all over sought out "the pink paper"! She traveled to multiple states to sell subscriptions. While she was gone, she learned that her good friend Thomas Moss had been lynched.

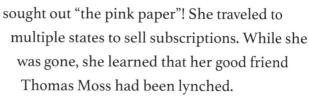

Mourning her dear friend and angered at what had happened, Ida Wells investigated lynching. She visited the sites of recent attacks, collected facts, and interviewed survivors. After she wrote an editorial for her paper, an angry mob burned down her newspaper's building.

Ida got a job writing for *The New York Age*. Her 1892 article about lynching sold ten thousand copies nationwide and more than one thousand in Memphis. Ida created a pamphlet called *Southern Horrors: Lynch Law in All Its Phases*. She challenged the reasons most whites gave for lynching and proposed that white men were killing Black people because they feared their political activity and economic success. Across the nation, women formed Ida B. Wells clubs to discuss lynching and advocate for equality.

When she was thirty-three, Ida moved to Chicago and married lawyer and newspaper owner Ferdinand Barnett. She bought into his newspaper, *The Chicago Conservator*, and continued writing. She took her first child, Charles, with her on speaking tours. She didn't like to cook, so her husband cooked dinner every night.

When a sheriff's negligence contributed to the lynching of an innocent Black man in Illinois, her son Charles talked her into going to advocate for justice. He said, "Mother, if you don't go, nobody else will." Because of her work, the judge punished the sheriff, and his decision helped end lynching in Illinois.

Ida B. Wells said, "The way to right wrongs is to turn the light of truth upon them." She did that her entire life, and it made a difference. By the time Ida died, lynching was rare. The abolitionist Frederick Douglass wrote a letter in support of her *Southern Horrors* pamphlet, saying:

The American-Canadian anti-slavery activist **Mary Ann Shadd Cary (1823–1893)** published and edited *The Provincial Freeman*, a Black newspaper. She was the first Black female publisher in North America and the second Black woman to earn a law degree.

"Brave woman! You have done your people and mine a service which can neither be weighed nor measured."

WRITE NOW

What problem do you need to investigate? Who can you interview to find out the truth?

WRITE TO KNOW

How to conduct an interview:

1. Research your subject.
2. Set a goal. What do you want to get out of the interview?
3. Brainstorm questions. The best questions allow the subject to answer in their own way.
4. Set up the interview.
5. Record. Take notes and use the recording to fill in details.
6. Listen and ask. Listen closely, and ask follow-up questions.
7. Pause. Did you get what you needed? Before the interview ends, ask, "Is there anything else you'd like to tell me?"
8. Review and rest. Review the transcript, and then let the interview sit for a few days before writing the story.

Journalist, editor, and social activist **Jovita Idár (1885–1946)** left teaching to become a writer and social activist, joining her father's paper, *La Crónica* (*The Chronicle*). In her writing, she fought for the education and civil rights of Mexican Americans and women. She wrote, "Educate a woman, and you educate a family."

Nellie Bly

Undercover Reporter, 1864–1922

Write to Expose:
Ten Days in a Madhouse

Nellie stared at herself in the mirror, practicing the blank look she hoped would get her committed to a women's psychiatric hospital. It did. Reporter Nellie Bly was determined to expose the hospital's abuses. She was pioneering a type of investigative journalism that her peers called "stunt reporting."

Born Elizabeth Jane Cochran in a small town in Western Pennsylvania, she was known more for her "riotous conduct" and "wild antics" than for her scholarship.

When Elizabeth was twenty, she became outraged when a columnist from the *Pittsburgh Dispatch* railed against working women, calling them "a monstrosity." Elizabeth wrote a fiery letter, advocating for women who took jobs to support their families. The editor asked her to write an article about the topic, and she did.

I said I could and I would. And I did.

—*Nellie Bly*

Pleased with her story, the editor gave her a job and the name "Nellie Bly," after a famous song. At the time, female journalists wrote only about women's issues. Nellie grew bored with the work and moved to New York City to write for a bigger paper.

Only, no one would hire her. So she wrote an article about how newspaper editors discriminated against female writers. Nellie's story helped her land a job at the *New York World*.

Nellie's editor asked her to investigate complaints against a women's psychiatric hospital on Blackwell Island. Registering under the name Nellie Brown, she spent ten grueling days at the hospital. The nurses scrubbed her with old washrags and dumped three buckets of ice-cold water over her head. She was drugged and locked in her room at night. When she emerged, her two-part article documenting the extensive mistreatment of residents earned national attention and triggered an official investigation.

Nellie's successful story gained her a slew of new assignments. She went undercover to write about the unfair practices of employment agencies, a secret baby adoption ring, and enslaved white women working in a factory. Nellie also interviewed boxer John L. Sullivan at his training camp, suffragette Susan B. Anthony, and nine-year-old Helen Keller and her teacher, Annie Sullivan.

Longing for adventure, Nellie traveled around the globe, replicating the trip that Phileas Fogg took in Jules Verne's novel *Around the*

World in Eighty Days. Cosmopolitan magazine reporter Elizabeth Bisland took the same journey from the Western side. Nellie completed the journey in just seventy-two days, beating the record of the fictional character Fogg and arriving home before Bisland. The trip made Nellie Bly famous. People wore Nellie Bly souvenir hats and gloves, wrote with their Nellie Bly pens on Nellie Bly paper, and bought Nellie Bly horse feed.

Fame meant that Nellie could no longer go undercover. She married, and when her husband died, she took over his manufacturing company. True to her values, Nellie improved working conditions for employees. Toward the end of her life, Nellie returned to journalism, writing articles to help the poor and disenfranchised.

WRITE TO KNOW

Here's how to discover your own big story:

1. Observe. Watch and listen for complaints, questions, or rumors.
2. Read. Look for stories that suggest a pattern, leave out key information, or spark your curiosity.
3. Investigate. Ask questions, read reports, and research inconsistencies.

When **Charles Dickens (1812–1870)** was just twelve, his father went to debtors prison and Charles left school to work in a boot-blacking factory. At fifteen, Charles took a job as an office boy for an attorney and reported on London's law courts, launching his career as a writer. Charles wrote *A Christmas Carol*, a story about ghosts who visit a stingy business owner. The story moved readers to give money to the poor.

WRITE NOW

Write an exposé.

1. Describe the problem and its causes.
2. Share attempts to solve the issue.
3. Propose your own solutions.

Where could you publish your story?

Elizabeth Bisland (1861–1929) was a poet, essayist, and prolific freelance writer. Before she landed her job at *Cosmopolitan*, Elizabeth wrote for four papers at the same time, racking up fifty thousand words a month and earning $5,000 a year. She hosted monthly arts salons at her New York City apartment.

THE WRITE STUFF

To avoid getting delayed by lost baggage, Nellie carried just a single bag packed with a silk blouse, cuffs and collars that matched her dress, handkerchiefs, a dressing gown and slippers, and a ghillie cap, which would later become associated with the character of Sherlock Holmes. She also packed lots of paper, pens, and ink.

Qiu Jin

Revolutionary, 1875–1907

Write to Revolutionize:
"A Respectful Proclamation
to China's 200 Million
Women Comrades"

Qiu Jin wanted to be a heroine like the girls she read about in books, warrior Hua Mulan and French fighter Joan of Arc. But she worried that her dream was impossible: "It's difficult to exchange a woman's headdress for a helmet."

Qiu Jin grew up in a wealthy, educated family. She learned how to read and write, ride horses, use a sword, practice archery, and perform martial arts. Her family often gathered together to read and write poetry.

But Qiu couldn't escape society's rules and roles for girls. In the tradition of the time, when she turned seven, the bones of her feet were broken and tightly bound to keep them tiny. Qiu's mother taught her sewing and embroidery to prepare for marriage.

Qiu was riveted by her country's political situation. The long-ruling Qing dynasty was crumbling. Foreigners colonized China, taking parcels of land. During the Boxer Rebellion, the people who opposed foreign influence killed hundreds of missionaries and Chinese Christians. Qiu watched with impatience—she wanted to serve her country.

In 1903, Qiu moved with her husband and two children to Beijing. She read about feminism and connected with women interested in politics. Intent on attending school, she sold her jewelry and purchased a ferry ticket to Japan. Because women could not travel alone, she unbound her feet, wore men's clothes, and carried a dagger.

When **Amani al-Khatahtbeh (1992–)** was seventeen years old, she developed the online magazine MuslimGirl.com to give Muslim women a platform to share their stories. In an interview with *Teen Vogue*, al-Khatahtbeh said, "It also became my way of asserting my narrative as an American Muslim to the public and reclaiming my identity."

Once in Japan, she enrolled in school and joined a group known as the Triad, which advocated for political change. Qiu soon became the primary editor and writer for the journal *Baihua Bao* (*Colloquial Magazine*). In one issue, she published a manifesto entitled "A Respectful Proclamation to China's 200 Million Women Comrades." She encouraged women to claim their power in the world:

> *I would now . . . rouse women's essence, spirit, to rise as birds in flight over fields, leaving swiftly earth's dust, that they may speedily cross the frontier into the great world of light and brilliance. I desire that they be leaders, awakened lions; advance messengers of learning and intelligence; that they may serve as rafts crossing cloudy ferries; as lamps in dark chambers.*

Don't tell me women / are not the stuff of heroes.

—Qiu Jin

Qiu and her group were planning a revolution. Qiu became head of Datung College of Physical Culture, a school for physical education teachers. Qiu used the school to train revolutionaries, running military drills. She referred to herself as the "female knight-errant of Mirror Lake." She was finally fulfilling her childhood wish to become a heroine.

Qiu Jin published a magazine with a friend and fellow poet. She wrote in a simple literary style and inspired many. Because the journal was controversial, the authorities shut it down after just two issues.

Blogger and podcast host **Scarlett Curtis (1995–)** curated the anthology *Feminists Don't Wear Pink and Other Lies*, a collection of essays by artists, activists, and celebrities about what feminism means to them. Her next anthology, *It's Not OK to Feel Blue and Other Lies*, raised awareness of mental health issues. Equality Now awarded Scarlett the Changemaker Award for young activists.

When government leaders confronted Qiu at the college, she refused to back down and was arrested. She was tortured for information and beheaded a few days later. She wrote these words right before she died: "Autumn rain and autumn wind, fill my heart with sorrow." A statue at her grave was inscribed with a single word: *heroine*.

WRITE TO KNOW

Qiu Jin was an eloquent speaker and wrote about the benefits of public speaking, including the following: leaders can speak anywhere; many can listen at no cost; anyone could understand; and leaders can motivate and organize listeners. What would you add?

WRITE NOW

A zine is an independently produced publication, often just a single folded sheet of paper, created to promote ideas or art. What ideas would you promote in a zine? Name, design, and create a zine to support an issue you care about.

Mary McLeod Bethune

Educator, 1875–1955

Write to Inspire:
"Last Will and Testament"

Mary McLeod grew up picking cotton on her family's farm. Her parents had been enslaved and saved money to buy the small farm. Mary was the fifteenth of seventeen children and the first to be born free. She also helped her mother deliver clean laundry to wealthy neighbors.

At one delivery stop, Mary entered a playhouse and saw pencils, slates, and books. Mary examined a book, and a white girl said, "You can't read that—put that down." Later, Mary wrote, "When she said that to me, it just did something to my pride and to my heart. . . . I went away from there determined to learn how to read." A missionary told the family about a new school for Black children, and Mary leapt at the chance to go.

The whole world opened to me when I learned to read.

—*Mary McLeod Bethune*

Italian physician **Maria Tecla Artemisia Montessori (1870–1952)** developed an educational process that encouraged children to explore their environment and work together. She wrote many books, pamphlets, and articles, and her ideas are used in schools all over the world.

Every Sunday, Mary gathered the farm children and taught them the poetry and songs she'd learned at school. Mary loved helping others. When people were sick in the community, she asked her mother to make soup. When a child needed shoes, Mary wanted to share her own.

A teacher helped Mary win a scholarship to boarding school. Mary embraced learning and social activities, participating in the chorus and the debating team. She earned her room and board by working in the laundry and kitchen. Her classmates called Mary a "peacemaker" and asked her for advice and comfort, especially when they were homesick.

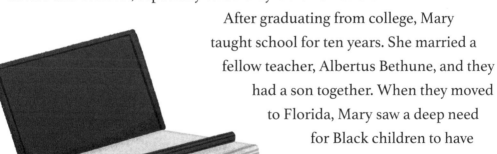

After graduating from college, Mary taught school for ten years. She married a fellow teacher, Albertus Bethune, and they had a son together. When they moved to Florida, Mary saw a deep need for Black children to have their own schools. She established the Daytona Normal and Industrial Institute for Negro Girls with just $1.50 and six young students.

Over the next twenty years, Mary grew the school into a high school and then Bethune-Cookman College, one of the first places in the South that a Black student could get a college education. Mary stayed on as the first president.

Sculptor **Augusta Savage (1892–1962)** opened her own school in Harlem, the Savage School of Arts and Crafts. She created a large piece for the New York World's Fair, called *Lift Every Voice and Sing*, and wrote stories for children.

While working in Daytona, Mary noticed that Black people needed better places to get medical care. She founded a small hospital that saved many lives in the twenty years it was open. The organization was praised for helping community members during the 1918 influenza outbreak.

After leaving Bethune-Cookman College, Mary worked with several organizations to help Black people get education, health care, and the right to vote. She became the president of the National Association of Colored Women and created the National Council of Negro Women to train Black women to be agents for social change. Mary also became the first Black woman to head a federal agency. She was determined to make a difference:

For I am my mother's daughter, and the drums of African skill beat in my heart. They will not let me rest while there is a single Negro boy or girl without a chance to prove his worth.

Near the end of her life, Mary wrote "My Last Will and Testament" to inspire others. She recounted nine "principles and policies" that she valued, including love, hope, faith, and confidence in one another. She ended her testimony with these words:

> *If I have a legacy to leave my people, it is my philosophy of living and serving. As I face tomorrow, I am content, for I think I have spent my life well. I pray now that my philosophy may be helpful to those who share my vision of a world of Peace, Progress, Brotherhood, and Love.*

WRITE NOW

In school yearbooks, kids gift values and artifacts to students in younger grades. What item, idea, or attitude would you give to family members or friends to help them with their lives? Create a list of virtues and values to give away.

WRITE TO CREATE

What image or saying reflects your life philosophy? Design and create a sign or T-shirt that shares your message.

Zitkála-Šá

Writer, Translator,
and Advocate,
1876–1938

Write to Honor:
Old Indian Legends

As a little girl growing up on the Yankton Sioux reservation in South Dakota, Zitkála-Šá loved sitting by the fire, listening to the elders tell stories:

> *As each in turn began to tell a legend, I pillowed my head in my mother's lap; and lying flat upon my back, I watched the stars as they peeped down upon me, one by one. The increasing interest of the tale aroused me, and I sat up eagerly listening for every word.*

Named Gertie Eveline Falker by her Yankton Sioux mother and white father, Gertie loved exploring. When she wasn't learning to bead or helping her mother fetch water, Gertie roamed the hills with her friends. They ate sweet roots, told stories about heroic deeds, and chased their shadows.

When Gertie was eight, missionaries came to the reservation and took her to a Quaker boarding school in Indiana. Gertie wanted to go, but her mother argued against it. Gertie's older brother had attended an English school, and it changed him. The US government used these schools to force Native American children to learn to speak and act like white people, forbidding them from using their Native names and language.

At school, Gertie despised the rigid rules—teachers rang bells to indicate when students should wake, pray, and eat. She hid under the bed to escape getting her hair cut, but the teachers found her: "I felt the cold blades of the scissors against my neck, and heard them gnaw off one of my thick braids. Then I lost my spirit."

Gertie struggled to fit in. Even so, she learned to read, write, and play the violin. After three years, she returned home, but didn't feel like her family understood her anymore. Teenage Gertie chose a new name for herself: Zitkála-Šá, Lakota for Red Bird.

Yearning for more education, Zitkála-Šá returned to the same Quaker boarding school, studied piano and violin, and taught other students. Against her mother's wishes, she enrolled in college. She began gathering the elders' stories and translating them into English for children.

As a senior, Zitkála-Šá won her college's speech contest with a talk championing equal opportunities for Native Americans. At the statewide tournament, students hung a large banner covered with racial slurs and a drawing of a Native American girl. Zitkála-Šá wrote: "Such worse than barbarian

Author, artist, and educator **Dame Kāterina Mataira (1932–2011)** revived the Māori language for her people, who live on an island off the coast of New Zealand. Because of her work, the students of the Māori can still learn, read, and write in their native language.

rudeness embittered me." She won a prize for her speech and became even more determined to honor and advocate for her culture.

After college, Zitkála-Šá wanted to help her people and took a job teaching music at Carlisle Indian School in Pennsylvania. She took her students to perform at the White House and published autobiographical stories. Through her teaching and writing, Zitkála-Šá openly opposed the school's practice of preventing students from nurturing their Native American heritage. The school's founder fired her.

Native American land rights activist and environmentalist **Winona LaDuke (1959–)** is an Anishinaabekwe (Ojibwe) enrolled member of the Mississippi Band Anishinaabeg. She's written many books, including *Recovering the Sacred: The Power of Naming and Claiming* (2005), about traditional beliefs and practices of Native Americans.

After briefly studying at the New England Conservatory of Music, Zitkála-Šá returned to the reservation to take care of her ailing mother and finish her book. *Old Indian Legends* was published in 1901, making Zitkála-Šá one of the first Native American women to publish traditional stories.

Zitkála-Šá became a prominent speaker and national policy advocate for Native American rights and culture. She spoke in traditional Sioux attire, which intrigued her audience and made them reconsider their stereotypes about Native people. Zitkála-Šá wanted Native Americans to have the right to vote and access to education and health care. She founded the National Council of American Indians and regularly testified before Congress.

She also raised awareness through her writing. Zitkála-Šá's book *Oklahoma's Poor Rich Indians* pushed Congress to pass the Indian

> **I loved best the evening meal, for that was the time old legends were told.**
>
> *—Zitkála-Šá*

Reorganization Act of 1934, which returned land to tribes and encouraged them to establish self-government of their lands.

Zitkála-Šá preserved the stories she had treasured as a child. In her writing and speaking, she also told her own stories—capturing the hearts of a whole new generation.

WRITE TO KNOW

"Once upon a time . . ." "Did you hear the one about . . . ?" "On a dark and stormy night . . ." What's your favorite way to start a story?

WRITE NOW

What stories would you like to save before they disappear? What family traditions do you want to preserve—a recipe, poem, celebration, or festival? Talk to the elders in your family or community. How can you record and preserve their traditions and stories for future generations?

Helen Keller

Author and Activist, 1880–1968

Write to Reveal:
The Story of My Life

Helen Keller spoke her first words when she was just six months old. But at nineteen months, Helen got very sick. When her fever broke, she could not see or hear. Helen's parents took her to specialists, but no one could restore her sight or hearing.

Helen quickly figured out how to get what she needed. By the time she was seven, Helen had invented almost sixty hand signs—like sucking her thumb when she wanted her baby sister. When Helen couldn't get her family to understand her, she kicked and screamed until she was exhausted. Some relatives suggested her parents send her to live in an institution.

> **I resolved that whatever role I did play in life, it would not be a passive one.**
>
> —*Helen Keller*

Helen's mother knew her daughter was bright. The family hired Annie Sullivan, a recent graduate of the Perkins School for the Blind, to be Helen's tutor. Annie was appalled that the family allowed Helen to grab food from anyone's plates. Annie and Helen moved to a tiny cottage on the property, where Annie hand-spelled words into Helen's hands day and night. Three weeks later, Annie ran water over Helen's hands and hand-spelled "water." Helen finally understood that the letters meant something. Annie had helped Helen unlock the key to language.

Helen attended Perkins and learned to read using Braille. In books, Helen could experience new worlds and ideas without depending on Annie to translate them for her. Helen worked hard to get into college, where she discovered her love for writing. *The Ladies' Home Journal* invited Helen to write her life story for the magazine. At twenty-one, Helen published her autobiography, *The Story of My Life*.

In 1904, Helen graduated from Radcliffe College, the first blind and deaf student to do so. After college, she wrote a groundbreaking article for *Ladies' Home Journal* about preventing blindness in infants. Helen wrote several books, though she considered writing challenging: "When I remember the books I have written, it is with pain, not joy; for I cannot forget the stern labor that went into them."

Helen wanted to spend her life advocating for others. But first she needed to overcome her fear of public speaking. As a deaf woman, she'd never heard her own voice and worried how she sounded to others. Helen took voice lessons to strengthen her speaking voice. She spent many hours writing, memorizing, and practicing her talk. Helen gave her first speech in 1913 and wrote this about the experience:

> *Terror invaded my flesh, my mind froze, my heart stopped beating. I kept repeating, "What shall I do? What shall I do to calm this tumult within me?"*

Robert J. Smithdas (1925–2014) was the second person who was deaf and blind to earn a bachelor's degree and the first to earn a master's degree. Smithdas wrote three books of poetry, including *City of Heart*. He taught at the Helen Keller National Center for Deaf-Blind Youths and advocated for deaf-blind education and employment.

Helen overcame her stage fright. For the next fifty years, she traveled around the world, raising money and educating people about blindness. She founded Helen Keller International to fight the causes of blindness. She advocated for the rights of blind people, including getting Braille adopted as their official language.

Helen also worked for the rights of all people. She cofounded the American Civil Liberties Union and created a charity to help veterans.

Disability activist **Alice Wong (1974–)** founded the Disability Visibility Project to amplify the voices of disabled people. The project collects oral histories through StoryCorps, publishes original essays, and provides education and support for writers with disabilities.

Helen never let being blind and deaf stop her from thinking big: "Blindness has no limiting effect upon mental vision. My intellectual horizon is infinitely wide. The universe it encircles is immeasurable."

WRITE NOW

Think about something you would love to do that seems beyond your reach. Write a story about how you might blast through physical or emotional obstacles to reach your goal. Use superpowers, real or imagined!

Mark Twain (1835–1910)—the pen name of Samuel Clemens—was an American writer and lecturer known best for his book *The Adventures of Huckleberry Finn.* Helen Keller met Mark Twain when she was fourteen, and they remained close friends until he died. She later wrote, "He never made me feel that my opinions were worthless, as so many people do. He knew that we do not think with eyes and ears."

Zora Neale Hurston

Novelist and Anthropologist,
1891–1960

Write to Preserve:
Mules and Men

Young Zora Hurston perched in a chinaberry tree, telling stories to herself. She created adventures for the dolls she'd crafted out of junk, Miss Corn-Shuck, Reverend Door-Knob, and Spool People. In town, she'd hide under the porch of the local store, listening to the grown-ups tell stories.

Zora was raised in Eatonville, Florida, the first all-Black city in America. All four of her grandparents had been born enslaved. Her father was a Baptist preacher and sharecropper who became the mayor of Eatonville. Her mother was a former schoolteacher who told Zora to "jump at the sun."

Zora learned to read when she was very young, and she excelled at school. When she was thirteen, her mother died and her father married a younger woman. He sent Zora to boarding school, where she scrubbed stairs to pay for her room and meals. When the school year ended, her father didn't want her to come home.

Zora spent the next five years moving between the houses of relatives and friends. Finally, she landed a job working as assistant to the lead singer in a theater troupe. When the tour ended in Baltimore, she was twenty-six and desperate to go back to school. Zora presented herself as a sixteen-year-old to qualify for free public schooling.

After high school, Hurston attended Howard University and later, Barnard College, where she was the sole Black student. She found community with writers and artists who were a part of the Harlem Renaissance, a flourishing of Black art and culture in New York.

Wallace Thurman (1902–1934) worked as a magazine editor, publisher, ghostwriter, and writer. He was best known for the novel *The Blacker the Berry: A Novel of Negro Life* and the play *Harlem*. Wallace became the first Black man to read manuscripts for a major New York publishing house.

Zora juggled multiple projects in different disciplines. As a graduate student, she researched Black folklore. She created and staged plays from the folklore she collected, believing that drama was "pure [Black] expression." She also wrote essays and fiction. A publisher saw one of Zora's stories and asked if she had a novel. She said yes and spent the next nine weeks writing *Jonah's Gourd Vine*.

Research is formalized curiosity. It is poking and prying with a purpose.

—Zora Neale Hurston

With the help and encouragement of a patron and her professor, Zora returned to Florida to research and collect the stories she grew up hearing. She soon published *Mules and Men*. This was the first book to preserve Black American folktales, music, songs, children's games, and hoodoo, a form of spirituality created by enslaved Black Americans.

Zora was awarded a fellowship from the Guggenheim Foundation to support her research and writing. She traveled to Haiti, where she gathered stories for *Tell My Horse*, a second book of folklore, and wrote her novel *Their Eyes Were Watching God*. The story focuses on the life of a Black woman, which was unusual for its time.

Zora founded a drama school at Bethune-Cookman College and taught at multiple schools. She took many part-time jobs to pay the bills so she could do what she loved: capture Black life in words. She coached actors for the Federal Theater Project, cleaned for a wealthy Florida family, and took care of an elderly judge. Through it all, she wrote from her heart: "I have the nerve to walk my own way, however hard, in my search for reality, rather than climb upon the rattling wagon of wishful illusions."

For thousands of years, people have told all kinds of stories:

MYTHS: Stories that explain natural events, such as how the world was made or why earthquakes happen.

LEGENDS: Tales about people who are larger than life, like King Arthur or Helen of Troy.

FABLES: Stories that deliver a moral lesson.

FAIRY TALES: Tales about animals, fairies, and creatures who use magic.

FOLK TALES: Stories about beliefs and practices passed down over time.

WRITE NOW

Write an origin story for yourself, your family, or something you love. If you don't have the facts, don't worry—make them up. Play with different forms: How will your story differ if it's a fairy tale instead of a legend?

American novelist, poet, and activist **Alice Walker (1944–)** wrote *The Color Purple* and coined the word *womanist* to refer to feminists of color. In the 1970s, Alice researched Zora Neale Hurston and restored Zora's grave, giving her a marker with the fitting epitaph "A Genius of the South."

Langston Hughes

Poet, 1902–1967

Write to Dream:
"Dreams"

Langston Hughes lived in six different American cities before he was twelve. His grandmother raised him, telling him how her first husband had died fighting against slavery. Wearing his bullet-ridden shawl, she told stories about all of the ancestors who fought for freedom. She also took Langston to the library.

> *I was unhappy for a long time, and very lonesome, living with my grandmother. Then it was that books began to happen to me, and I began to believe in nothing but books and the wonderful world in books— where if people suffered, they suffered in beautiful language, not in monosyllables, as we did in Kansas.*

Langston Hughes started college in New York City during the Harlem Renaissance, a thriving cultural explosion of music, art, and writing. In the summer of 1926, Langston, Zora Neale Hurston, Countee Cullen, and Wallace Thurman founded a magazine called *Fire!*, designed to publish Black writers.

Longing to travel, Langston landed a job working on a ship bound for Africa. On the first night, he dumped a box of books overboard, saving only Walt Whitman's *Leaves of Grass*. He wrote:

> *It was like throwing a million bricks out of my heart—for it wasn't only the books that I wanted to throw away but . . . the memory of my father, the poverty and uncertainties of my mother's life, the stupidities of color prejudice, black in a white world, the fear of not finding a job.*

When Langston returned to study at Howard University, he worked as a busboy at a fancy Washington, DC, hotel. He noticed the poet Vachel Lindsay and placed his poems by the poet's plate, muttering praises for his work. At a poetry reading that night, Vachel read all three of Langston's poems, announcing that he'd discovered a new Black poet. The event was covered in newspapers across the country. Langston soon published his first book of poems, *The Weary Blues*.

Thanks to the patronage of a wealthy woman, Langston finished college and wrote his first novel, *Not Without Laughter*. His patron provided a monthly stipend and offered her advice and criticism of his writing. But the relationship

Vachel Lindsay (1879–1931) took multiple walking trips, trading dramatic poetry performances for food and lodging. He created modern singing poetry.

stifled Langston, and the friendship collapsed.

Langston wrote and performed his poetry for readers across the country, becoming the first Black American to earn a living as a writer and lecturer. He used the rhythm and cadence of words to capture the spirit and movement of Black music in his poems.

Walt Whitman (1819–1892) was a humanist, an advocate for a philosophy that values the goodness of humanity and seeks rational solutions to life's problems. Considered the father of free verse, Walt is best known for his collection *Leaves of Grass*.

Langston wanted his writing to inspire Black Americans to "hold fast to dreams." He created the character of Jesse B. Semple and wrote newspaper stories about the struggle to be a Black person in America. Through the Jesse Semple stories, Langston Hughes encouraged Black people to feel pride in themselves, just as his grandmother had done for him.

WRITE NOW

Langston Hughes wrote about holding on to dreams. What do you dream for your future self? Imagine your life five or ten years from now: What will you be doing? Where will you live? Who will you hang out with? Write about every aspect of your best possible future life. Write in the present tense and use lots of details.

> **My best poems were all written when I felt the worst. When I was happy, I didn't write anything.**
>
> —*Langston Hughes*

Lorraine Hansberry (1930–1965) was the first Black female playwright to have a play produced on Broadway. She borrowed a line from Langston Hughes's poem "Harlem" for *A Raisin in the Sun*: "What happens to a dream deferred? Does it dry up like a raisin in the sun?"

WRITE TO CREATE

Langston Hughes wrote about himself for an authors' dictionary:

> *I live in Harlem, New York City. I am unmarried. I like "Tristan," goats milk, short novels, lyric poems, heat, simple folk, boats and bullfights; I dislike "Aida," parsnips, long novels, narrative poems, cold pretentious folk, buses and bridges.*

Create your own bio using Hughes's description of himself as a model.

George Orwell

Novelist, 1903–1950

Write to Oppose:
Animal Farm

Born Eric Arthur Blair, George Orwell wrote his first poem before he was six. Often lonely, he made up stories and talked to imaginary friends. When he met his teenage love, Eric was standing on his head and said, "You are noticed more if you stand on your head than if you are right way up." The two wanted to become famous writers someday. They played a game called "Set Piece Poetry," where they chose a subject, words, and form and competed to write the best poem.

After serving five and a half years with the Indian Imperial Police in Burma, Eric resigned to become a writer. He disguised himself and wrote stories about people living in poverty. Worried that his work might embarrass his family, Eric changed his name to George Orwell before publishing his escapades in the book *Down and Out in Paris and London*.

George fought in the Spanish Civil War and was wounded in the throat by a sniper's bullet. Fighting in the war ignited a new purpose:

> ... *and every line of serious work that I have written since 1936 has been written, directly or indirectly, against totalitarianism and for democratic socialism, as I understand it. What I have most wanted to do ... is to make political writing into an art.*

George married Eileen in 1936, and they adopted a baby during World War II. Shortly after the war ended, George's wife died in surgery. He was devastated and immersed himself in work, publishing more than 110,000 words that year alone.

In 1945, George published his novel *Animal Farm*—a story about farm animals who rebel against their human farmer to create a society in which all the animals could be equal and happy. At the time, Americans worried that Communism would lead to the conditions George described, and the book sold well.

When George Orwell published the dystopian novel *Nineteen Eighty-Four* in 1949, he wanted to condemn bullies and champion the underdog. He believed that if people sought truth, they would be free from anyone who'd threaten to enslave them.

In the book George coined several terms that

Margaret Cavendish (1623–1673) was a philosopher and prolific writer who popularized ideas of the scientific revolution. Her book *The Blazing World* is considered the first science fiction novel. Margaret is famous for writing, "My much writing is a disease."

have become part of everyday vocabulary, such as *big brother*, *thought police*, and *newspeak*. His name was even made into an adjective, *Orwellian*, to refer to anything touched by totalitarianism, a dictatorial form of government that forbids individual freedom. *Nineteen Eighty-Four* has been translated into more than sixty-five languages and has sold tens of millions of copies. It has inspired plays, movies, music, and television shows.

WRITE TO KNOW

In *Nineteen Eighty-Four*, George Orwell created technological inventions that seem contemporary now. Telescreens provided entertainment and tracked users' movements. George also imagined Speakwrite, which converts speech into written text. Other writers have imagined the following:

- Rocket-powered space flight (*Comical History of the States and Empires of the Moon* by Cyrano de Bergerac, 1657)
- Submarines (*The Blazing World* by Margaret Cavendish, 1666)
- Helicopters, genetic cloning, virtual reality (*Brave New World* by Aldous Huxley, 1932)
- Bluetooth earbuds, flatscreen televisions, 24-hour banking machines (*Fahrenheit 451* by Ray Bradbury, 1953)
- Tablet computers (*2001: A Space Odyssey* by Arthur C. Clark, 1968)

Writer and philosopher **Aldous Leonard Huxley (1894–1963)** wrote more than fifty books in his lifetime. Inspired by H. G. Wells's utopian novels *A Modern Utopia* and *Men Like Gods*, Aldous set out to write a parody of Wells's work. Aldous's *Brave New World* envisioned a terrifying future.

WRITE NOW

George Orwell wrote his futuristic novels to oppose injustice. What lie or fact do you want to expose as leading to harmful conditions? Write a story set in the future that supports your vision.

WRITE TO CREATE

A pseudonym can help writers hide their true identity. To create pseudonyms, writers shorten their names, mine family names, or use words meaningful to them. Create your pseudonym.

English novelist **Rose Macaulay (1881–1958)** wrote twenty-three novels, including the dystopian novel *What Not*. She also wrote the satirical utopian novel *Orphan Island*. Rose and the writer Aldous Huxley traveled in the same literary circles, and some of her ideas show up in his novel *Brave New World*.

> When I sit down to write a book . . . there is some lie that I want to expose, some fact to which I want to draw attention, and my initial concern is to get a hearing.

—George Orwell

Rachel Carson

Marine Biologist and Environmentalist, 1907–1964

Write to Warn:
Silent Spring

Rachel Carson grew up on a farm overlooking the Allegheny River in Pennsylvania. Her mother taught her to love nature and stories. Rachel wrote her first story at eight and later said, "I can remember no time, even in earliest childhood, when I didn't assume I was going to be a writer."

In college, Rachel discovered her passion for nature. After earning a master's degree, she interviewed at the Bureau of Fisheries, and the director hired her to edit a radio script on sea life. He was so impressed with Rachel's writing that he gave her a full-time job as a junior aquatic biologist.

While working at the Bureau, Rachel wrote a poetic report about the sea, the creatures that live in it, and how they are interconnected in a web of life. Her boss urged her to send it to *The Atlantic* magazine. The story led to the publication of her first book, *Under the Sea Wind: A Naturalist's Picture of Ocean Life.*

> **If there is poetry in my book about the sea, it is not because I deliberately put it there, but because no one could write truthfully about the sea and leave out the poetry.**

—Rachel Carson

Rachel Carson's next book, *The Sea Around Us*, won the National Book Award for nonfiction and was on the bestseller list for eighty-six weeks. Because of her literary success, Rachel was able to resign from her job to write full-time.

During her years at the Bureau, Rachel had researched the pesticide DDT. Cheap and effective, DDT was sprayed in neighborhoods to eliminate Dutch elm disease in trees and was put in fabric to deter insects. American troops used DDT to eliminate lice and control malaria, typhus, and bubonic plague. The chemical was even put in furniture polish, paint, and fabric treatments.

Rachel grew increasingly concerned about how DDT was affecting the planet. The pesticide didn't just kill insects and weeds; it lived in the soil and water for fifteen years, poisoning plants, birds, animals, and fish. Rachel believed that DDT, stored in the

Rachel Carson's work spurred many positive legal actions, including:

- Clean Air Act (1963)
- Wilderness Act (1964)
- National Environmental Policy Act (1969)
- formation of the Environmental Protection Agency (1970)
- Clean Water Act (1972)
- Endangered Species Act (1972)
- EPA's ban of DDT (1972)
- Toxic Substances Control Act (1976)

Professor **Mary Temple Grandin (1947–)** writes about the humane treatment of animals. She's best known for documenting what it's like to live with autism, especially in her book *Thinking in Pictures*.

fat cells of animals and humans, caused cancer. She pitched an article about the chemical to *Reader's Digest*. They rejected it.

Rachel learned that *Reader's Digest* was going to publish an article about the benefits of DDT in killing gypsy moths, an invasive pest that consumes the leaves of trees and shrubs. Earlier that year Rachel received a letter from a friend, reporting that after a plane sprayed DDT to kill mosquitoes, she found dead songbirds.

In 1962, Rachel Carson published *Silent Spring*, her book warning the public about the effects of pesticides on the planet. Critics lashed out at her. Chemical companies accused her of being a "hysterical woman," a cat-loving spinster, and a communist. (Rachel did have a cat, named Jeffie, who curled up on her desk while she wrote.) One chemical company threatened to sue. Even the FBI investigated Rachel.

But the book was received well by much of the public and became a bestseller. Rachel got many invitations to speak and was interviewed widely. President John F. Kennedy

Poet and professor **Camille T. Dungy (1972–)** has written several award-winning books of poetry. To bring more Black writers into the conversation, she edited *Black Nature: Four Centuries of African American Nature Poetry*.

asked a group of scientists to investigate DDT. The report confirmed Rachel's argument, and new laws were passed banning its use.

Rachel's writing showed people the world was a giant connected ecosystem and helped ignite the environmental movement.

Swedish teenager **Greta Thunberg (2003–)** sailed to the United States to speak about slowing climate change at the United Nations Climate Summit. Her speech, featuring the refrain "How dare you?" has been set to music.

WRITE NOW

If you could warn the world about something, what would it be? Choose a problem that worries you and write a warning for others. How will you broadcast your message?

WRITE TO CREATE

Today people put warnings on food, on clothing, online, in letters, and in books. Create a warning label for yourself—or your friends and family members. Consider how and where you would display it. Could you create a sign for your bedroom door? Or print it on a hat or T-shirt?

Mary Garber

Sportswriter,
1916–2008

Write to Champion:
Twin City Sentinel

When Mary Garber was eight, she decided to become a newspaper reporter. She created the "Garber News" to mail to her grandparents, writing news stories about everything the family had been doing. No doubt, she included reports about playing tackle football on her neighborhood team. Later, Mary sharpened her writing skills by working on her high school and college newspapers.

When she graduated from college, Mary moved home to look for a newspaper job. Not many women worked at papers as writers, and it took her two years to land a job as society editor for the *Twin City Sentinel*. She found a way to highlight her love for sports, writing a column teaching women how to watch a live football game.

When most of the writers left to fight in World War II, Mary moved to the sports

department, and something clicked. But after the war, when male staff returned to the paper, Mary was sent back to the newsroom. She volunteered to write about sports until her boss finally assigned her to the sports page. For the next thirty years, Mary was the only woman writing about sports in the North Carolina area and one of the few female sportswriters in the country.

Mary covered games for the local orphanage, high schools, and colleges. She also wrote about games at Black high schools and traditionally Black colleges, becoming one of the first reporters to cover Black players. Mary wrote about the good in every person. Student athletes sought her out for advice because she listened well. "It's just a question of letting people know that you're interested and that you care about them," she explained.

When someone asked her if the schools minded that she was a woman, she said:

> *Well, the high school kids and the coaches were so delighted that somebody was coming around to cover them that I think I could have been a two-headed monkey and they wouldn't have cared.*

Women weren't allowed into the press box, so Mary covered games from the wives' box. When she was finally admitted, Mary wore a badge that said, "No Women and Children Allowed in the Press Box." She was also barred from entering the locker room. Some of the coaches would bring out players to talk to her. Once, she and an assistant coach listened to the coach's talk from the showers, getting doused with water in the process.

At first, Mary didn't know enough about high school and college football to cover a game. So she studied: Mary asked questions, read books, sat in on coaches' meetings, attended officials' clinics, and graduated from umpire school. Over her forty-five years on the paper, she covered football, basketball, baseball, swimming, tennis, golf, cross-country track, boxing, wrestling, soapbox derbies, marbles tournaments, and the steeplechase.

By the end of her life, Mary Garber had won nearly every major sports writing award. She became the first woman to win sports journalism's highest honor, the Red Smith Award. The athletes and coaches treasured Garber for shining a light on their efforts. One young boy identified her this way: "That's Miss Mary Garber. And she don't care who you are, if you do something, she'll write about you."

WRITE TO KNOW

Mary Garber offered this advice to young journalists:

- Get a good education.
- Read other newspapers.
- Don't be careless in your choice of words.
- Get as much critique of your work as possible.
- Check your quotes.

Stunt reporter **Winifred Sweet Black Bonfils (1863–1936)** wrote as Annie Laurie, posing as a vagrant to expose the harsh treatment of the poor in a San Francisco hospital. In 1892, she snuck into an all-men's club to watch a boxing match and became the first woman to cover a prizefight for an American newspaper.

WRITE NOW

Mary Garber recommended that young sportswriters practice by pretending to cover games. Find a game online or go to a live game, and take notes on each play. Write up your story. Check out how other journalists reported on the game. Which story is more readable? Why?

If you can't find a game to cover, write about an ordinary event, like how your family gets ready for dinner.

A major league scout saw **Wendell Smith (1914–1972)** pitch a winning game and told him that he couldn't sign him because he was Black. Wendell decided to help Black people play in the majors. He became a professional sportswriter and recommended that the Brooklyn Dodgers hire Jackie Robinson, who became major league baseball's first Black player.

There are good stories everywhere if you just open your eyes and see them.

—*Mary Garber*

Hans and Sophie Scholl

Social Activists, 1918–1943
and 1921–1943

Write to Critique:
The White Rose Pamphlets

Hans and Sophie Scholl grew up in a close-knit family in Germany that loved to discuss art, literature, and philosophy. They were raised to think critically and form their own opinions.

In 1933, Hitler became chancellor of Germany and promised that Nazi nationalism could help failing businesses and eliminate class distinctions. Believing that Hitler could improve German life, the Scholl children joined Nazi youth organizations, but quickly became disillusioned.

The leader of Hans's Hitler Youth group forbade him from reading books by Jewish writers. Sophie questioned why one of her Jewish friends couldn't join the league. Then a beloved teacher openly disagreed with Nazi ideals and was sent to a concentration camp.

The siblings joined anti-Nazi groups. With their friends, they created a small newsletter called *Windlicht* (*Storm Lantern*) and published their poems and articles with hidden anti-Nazi messages.

During his service as a medic, Hans witnessed Nazi cruelty to Jewish people. When he got to medical school in Munich, he was ready to resist. Sophie joined Hans at the university and discovered under a desk a leaflet that read, "Adopt passive resistance . . . wherever you are." She rushed to her brother's room, where she found evidence of his involvement in creating the flier. Sophie confronted Hans—resisting the Nazis was dangerous. Despite her worries, she joined the effort.

Hans Scholl and a friend wrote leaflets that criticized National Socialism and the killing of Jewish people. They encouraged readers to resist the Nazi regime for spiritual reasons. They wrote: "We will not be silent. We are your bad conscience. The White Rose will not leave you in peace!"

On the morning of February 18, 1943, Hans and Sophie took a suitcase full of leaflets to the university. They entered the large inner courtyard and deposited leaflets on windowsills and in front of doors. Just as lectures were dismissed, Sophie tossed the last bunch of leaflets over a balcony railing. A janitor saw them, and the two were arrested.

We will not be silent.

—*The White Rose youth*

After eighteen hours of interrogation, Hans and Sophie Scholl confessed, taking sole responsibility for the creation and distribution of the leaflets. The police discovered the draft of a seventh pamphlet, written by a member of their group. The three were convicted of high treason and executed days later.

After Hans's death, someone discovered his father's favorite words from the German poet Johann Wolfgang von Goethe written on his cell wall: "Despite all the powers closing in, hold yourself up."

Shortly before her death, Sophie Scholl is reported to have said, "What difference does my death make if our actions arouse thousands of people? The students will definitely rise up."

The White Rose youth wrote seven leaflets. After their deaths, Allied planes scattered the pamphlets over Germany. Their words brought hope to people in occupied Europe, prison cells, and even concentration camps. Somehow, a leaflet made its way to America, and an editorial in the *New York Times* honored the young martyrs:

> *These Munich students, few or many, representative or otherwise, rose gloriously . . . protesting in the name of principles which Hitler thought he had killed forever. In years to come we, too, may honor [them].*

Anna Politkovskaya (1958–2006) was a journalist and human rights activist from Chechnya who told stories about the Second Chechen War that revealed human rights abuses, the silencing of the press, and the government's lies. She was assassinated on October 7, 2006, just after finishing her final book, *A Russian Diary*.

WRITE TO KNOW

Sophie and Hans Scholl used pamphlets to critique the government's policies. Today, protesters use established media, like newspapers and online magazines, as well as blogs and social media platforms, to voice their criticism. Other forms include editorials, letters to the editor, political cartoons, videos, memes, or tweets. Can you think of other ways to publicize a critique?

Jewish poet **Ilse Aichinger (1921–2016)** was living in Vienna during World War II. When she saw a poster about the White Rose, she wrote: "As I read those names, an inexpressible hope leaped up in me. . . . This hope . . . was life itself . . . speaking to us through the death of the Scholls and their companions. You can live without owning anything. . . . You can't live without hope."

WRITE NOW

If you created a campaign to critique a policy in your school, community, or government, what would it be about? What form would it take? Choose a topic and create a critique document.

James Baldwin

Novelist, 1924–1987

Write to Educate:
*Go Tell It
on the Mountain*

James Baldwin grew up in Harlem. When he was three, his mother married a Baptist Pentecostal minister who gave James his surname, as well as brutal beatings. James recalled: "My father said . . . I was the ugliest boy he had ever seen." James described himself as having a forehead that was wrinkled like a bulldog and eyes that bulged like a bullfrog.

Behind those eyes, James had a powerful mind determined to learn. Starting at age ten, a series of mentors stepped up, discussed books with James, and introduced him to movies and museums. His French teacher, the Black poet Countee Cullen, encouraged him to join the high school literary club. James haunted the library and read constantly:

> *In those days my mother was given to the exasperating and mysterious habit of having babies. As they were born, I took them over with one hand and held a book with the other.*

At fourteen, James was attracted to both boys and girls. He feared becoming undone by drugs and alcohol. James threw himself into his faith, becoming an apprentice minister while still a teenager. Once again, James found comfort in books:

> *You think your pain and heartbreak are unprecedented in the history of the world, but then you read. It was books that taught me that the things that tormented me the most were the very things that connected me with all the people who were alive or who had ever been alive.*

After winning a grant to work on his autobiography, James moved to Paris. He struggled to make enough money to live and write. After eight years, James finally finished a novel based on his own life, titled *Go Tell It on the Mountain*. It was published to rave reviews and has never gone out of print.

James was happy living in Paris. Then he saw a photo of a Black teen being harassed by a mob of white people as she walked to school. James knew he needed to write about the civil rights movement.

Novelist, poet, and children's writer **Countee Cullen (1903–1946)** embraced a classic English style of poetry, believing it would build bridges with the white community. His books *Color* and *The Black Christ and Other Poems* explore themes of race and heritage.

He met Martin Luther King Jr. and appeared with Malcolm X. He helped organize the March on Washington.

James Baldwin did some of his most important writing during this period. He interviewed others, examined his own life, and dug deeply for the truth:

> But it is part of the business of the writer—as I see it—to examine attitudes, to go beneath the surface, to tap the source.

James understood that justice for Black people was connected to issues of class, gender, and sexuality. He believed his life's mission was to bear witness to the truth, to help people understand the civil rights movement. Today, James's legacy endures as a powerful witness for justice.

WRITE NOW

James Baldwin said, "Go back to where you started or as far back as you can, examine all of it, travel your road again and tell the truth about it." Make a timeline of your life, noting the experiences that have shaped who you are today. Choose one of these experiences and write it!

WRITE TO CREATE

Artists like Nick Cave, who makes bodysuits, and Shinique Smith, who creates mixed-media pieces from accessories and clothing, demonstrate

Novelist and poet **Richard Wright (1908–1960)** didn't attend school regularly until he was thirteen and published his first story at age fifteen. He mentored James Baldwin early in his career. Richard moved to Paris in 1946 and became a French citizen, writing four thousand haiku poems in the last years of his life.

that what we wear reflects how we see ourselves. Draw or collage an item of clothing, an accessory, or a complete look that reflects who you are.

On the one-hundredth anniversary of the Emancipation Proclamation, James Baldwin wrote about racial injustice in a letter to his fifteen-year-old nephew; it is included in his book *The Fire Next Time*. Inspired by James's book, journalist and author **Ta-Nehisi Paul Coates (1975–)** wrote the book *Between the World and Me*, a letter to his teenage son about what it means to be Black in America.

You write in order to change the world, knowing perfectly well that you probably can't, but also knowing that literature is indispensable to the world. . . . The world changes according to the way people see it, and if you alter, even but a millimeter, the way people look at reality, then you can change it.

—*James Baldwin*

Malcolm X

Activist, 1925–1965

Write to Ignite:
The Autobiography
of Malcolm X

Malcolm Little tagged along to his father's speeches, hearing him say, "Up, you mighty race. You can accomplish what you will!" Malcolm's father received multiple death threats from a white supremacist organization, and someone burned down their home. When Malcolm was six, his father was run over by a trolley. The family believed he'd been killed by people who disagreed with his message.

Malcolm's mother tried to keep the family together, but eventually he and his siblings were sent to separate foster homes. Malcolm remembered his father's words and studied hard. When he declared that he wanted to be a lawyer, his favorite teacher told him it wasn't "a realistic career" for a Black person.

At fourteen, Malcolm moved to his half-sister's home in Boston. He joined a gang that robbed apartments, got caught, and was sentenced to ten years in prison. While he was in jail, Malcolm's siblings told him about

Elijah Muhammad, cofounder of the Nation of Islam (NOI), a religious and political movement that believes in the superiority of the African race. Malcolm wrote to Elijah and learned about the movement from his letters.

Malcolm was frustrated by his inability to express his thoughts in writing. He borrowed a dictionary from a fellow prisoner and copied pages to learn new words. Malcolm would later say that his alma mater was books:

> *I have often reflected upon the new vistas that reading opened to me. . . . My homemade education gave me, with every additional book that I read, a little bit more sensitivity to the deafness, dumbness, and blindness that was afflicting the black race in America.*

Before he left prison, Malcolm denounced the name Little as a slave name and claimed "X," representing a lost tribal name. Malcolm became a spirited speaker for the Nation of Islam. He taught that the success of Black people depended on staying separate and demanding equal rights, using force only to defend against violent attacks.

Malcolm advocated for a clean lifestyle and urged his followers to give up smoking, drinking, drug use, stealing, and other criminal activity. When he discovered that his mentor wasn't following the rules of Islam, he broke with the organization. He delved into studying Islam and took a hajj, a pilgrimage to Mecca.

In Mecca, Malcolm spoke with Muslims from multiple races and developed new beliefs about integration: "True Islam removes racism, because people of all colors and races who accept its religious principles . . . accept each other as brothers and sisters."

Malcolm changed his name to El-Hajj Malik el-Shabazz and shared his new message. Then he began receiving death threats.

On February 14, 1965, someone threw a firebomb through the front window of Malcolm's home in Queens, New York, where he was sleeping with his wife and four daughters. It damaged the home, but the family escaped unharmed. A week later, Malcolm went to Manhattan's Audubon Ballroom to speak. Three men stormed the stage, shooting and killing Malcolm X.

Before he died, Malcolm dictated his life story to writer Alex Haley. Published in 1965, *The Autobiography of Malcolm X* was praised by critics and banned widely. The book has sold millions of copies, has been released in more than forty-five editions, and has been translated into many languages. The Library of Congress included the book on its list of one hundred books that shaped America.

After a successful career in the Coast Guard, **Alex Haley (1921–1992)** began writing about prominent Black people. He credited Malcolm X for his transition into writing books. His Pulitzer Prize–winning book *Roots* (1976) recounted his ancestors' journey from Africa to America as enslaved persons.

WRITE TO KNOW

Malcolm X changed his mind about big ideas. Questioning helps thinkers discover new theories and

People don't realize how a man's whole life can be changed by one book.

—*Malcolm X*

create innovative solutions to problems. Write a list of questions you might use to challenge ideas, theories, and beliefs. Start with the best question words ever: *why* and *how*. Move on to *Why not?* and *How come?*

WRITE NOW

In his autobiography, Malcolm X stated that most adults failed because they were afraid to try: "Children have a lesson adults should learn, to not be ashamed of failing, but to get up and try again." Write about a time when you failed and tried again. How could sharing your story help others overcome fear?

Scholar-artist-activist **Dr. Su'ad Abdul Khabeer (1978–)** founded Sapelo Square, an online resource for the Black Muslim community in the United States, launching it on Malcolm X's ninetieth birthday. Through performances, scholarship, and her book *Muslim Cool: Race, Religion, and Hip Hop in the United States*, Su'ad explores the connections between race and popular culture.

Jan Morris

Author and Historian, 1926–2020

Write to Explore: *Conundrum*

As a young child, Jan Morris experienced a conundrum. Assigned male and called James at birth, she remembered sitting under the piano while her mother played: "I was three or perhaps four years old when I realized that I had been born into the wrong body, and should really be a girl." Jan "cherished this as a secret" for twenty years.

Jan felt different from other children. When her two older brothers left for school, she spent hours by herself wandering the hills around her house, watching ships through her telescope. She wrote:

> *The instrument played an important part in my fancies and conjectures, perhaps because it seemed to give me a private insight into distant worlds, and when at the age of eight or nine I wrote the first pages of a book, I called it* Travels with a Telescope, *not a bad title at that.*

In her late teens, Jan joined the 9th Queens Royal Lancers and worked as a spy. She never felt at home in the army, thinking of herself as a "stranger and imposter." But the experience gave her the opportunity to learn how to examine the world around her:

> *For myself, I think I learnt my trade largely in the 9th Lancers, for I developed in that regiment an almost anthropological interest in the forms and attitudes of its society; and sitting there undetected, so to speak, I evolved the techniques of analysis and observation that I would later adapt to the writer's craft.*

After the army, Jan delved into reporting. In 1953, *The Times* assigned her to cover Edmund Hillary and Tenzing Norgay as they attempted to be the first to summit Mount Everest, the world's highest mountain. Jan climbed thousands of feet above base camp so that when the explorers reached the top, she could race to the bottom and phone in the scoop.

In 1956, Jan received a fellowship to travel and write. She visited every state in the United States and wrote the book *Coast to Coast*. She went on to write about many more places, including *The World of Venice* (1960) and *The Presence of Spain* (1965). Jan became known for

Lisa Bunker (1962–) was elected to represent her town in the New Hampshire House of Representatives as one of her state's first transgender representatives. Lisa has written two novels for young people, including *Felix Yz* and *Zenobia July*, a story about a trans-girl tackling a cyber mystery.

portraying the personality of places, describing their characteristics with rich language.

As Jan tackled one of her biggest professional projects, a three-volume history of the British Empire, she also explored her lifelong conundrum. Because how she felt on the inside (her gender identity) didn't match the sex she was assigned at birth, Jan's feeling of being born in the wrong body never left her. She described gender as being "the essentialness of oneself." And as long as she lived as a man, she felt out of sync with herself. At this time, Jan began transitioning from male to female. She chronicled this process in her book, *Conundrum*:

Raquel Willis (1990/1991–) started her career as a newspaper reporter but felt called to work as an activist. While working for the Transgender Law Center, Raquel founded *Black Trans Circles* to create healing spaces for Black trans women and organize efforts to address anti-trans violence. She writes for many publications and was the first Black transgender person to be executive editor of *Out* magazine.

> *To myself I had been a woman all along, and I was not going to change the truth of me, only discard the falsity. . . . I embarked upon it only with a sense of thankfulness, like a lost traveler finding the right road at last.*

Jan wrote for the rest of her life, publishing more than forty books. She answered all of her mail and penned encouraging notes to aspiring writers: "Don't worry about rejection slips, everyone gets them. Experience everything."

WRITE NOW

Jan Morris wrote literary portraits of places, describing their personalities. Write a description of a place you know well, or create a fictional world you'd love to visit. How is the place like a person? What characteristics does it have?

Kacen Callender (1989–) is the author of several novels for young people, including *Hurricane Child*. Growing up in the Caribbean, Kacen experienced cultural anti-queerness. As an adult who identifies as Black, queer, and trans, Kacen said, "I think this put me on a mission to help heal young queer readers, to let them know that they aren't alone, and to give them hope."

WRITE TO CREATE

Jan Morris used uncommon and interesting words, like "gallimaufry" (a confused jumble of things). Writers of haiku create a saijiki, a list of favorite seasonal words, to help them write poems. Create your own word list—collect your favorite words or gather terms for a project.

> **I resist the idea that travel writing has got to be factual. I believe in its imaginative qualities and its potential as art and literature.**
>
> —*Jan Morris*

Patsy Takemoto Mink

Lawyer and Politician, 1927–2002

Write to Legislate: *Title IX*

Can thirty-seven words change the world?

Patsy Mink wrote Title IX, a thirty-seven-word federal civil rights law, so that future generations wouldn't have to fight so hard to achieve their dreams.

Patsy Takemoto Mink grew up in Hawaii, a third-generation Japanese American. After an appendectomy at age four, Patsy decided to become a doctor. As a young girl, she sat in a tree and read books out loud.

When she arrived at the University of Nebraska, Patsy discovered that the school's policy forbade students of color from living in the dorms. Patsy held a letter-writing campaign and successfully lobbied to end this practice.

After earning degrees in zoology and chemistry, Patsy applied to twelve medical schools and was rejected by all of them because she was a woman. A mentor suggested she try law school, and Patsy was accepted to the University of Chicago as a foreign student. At the school's International

House, Patsy met geology student and World War II veteran John Mink. They married and had a daughter, Gwendolyn (Wendy).

After graduating, Patsy and John moved back to Hawaii. She got involved in the Democratic Party and ran for office. She became the first Japanese American woman elected to the territorial legislature and later the territorial senate. She wrote the "equal pay for equal work" law and advocated for improving the educational system.

From the Title IX law:
No person in the United States shall, on the basis of sex, be excluded from participation in, be denied the benefits of, or be subjected to discrimination under any education program or activity receiving Federal financial assistance.

In 1959, when Hawaii became a state, Patsy ran for the House of Representatives and was defeated in the primary. Five years later, she won and became the first woman of color, the first Japanese American, and the first Hawaiian woman elected to Congress. She served six consecutive terms.

In 1972, Representative Patsy Mink and Senator Birch Bayh from Indiana wrote and presented Title IX, an amendment to the Higher Education Act, which prohibits institutions that receive federal funding from discriminating against people because of their gender.

> We have to build things that we want to see accomplished, in life and in our country, based on our own personal experiences . . . to make sure that others . . . do not have to suffer the same discrimination.

—*Patsy Takemoto Mink*

Athletic directors protested, fearing a loss of funding for popular men's sports. Opponents to Title IX proposed the Casey Amendment, which would allow schools to choose whether to provide equal funding for athletic programs. Patsy lobbied fiercely against the amendment. Just before the vote, she received a phone call that her daughter had been in a serious car accident. She left immediately, and the Casey Amendment passed by one vote.

> In 1969, **Shirley Anita Chisholm (1924–2005)** became the first Black woman elected to Congress. Known as "Fighting Shirley," she sponsored legislation that funded extending hours of daycare facilities and guaranteed a minimum annual income for families. She wrote, "If I speak and write easily now, that early education is the main reason."

When Patsy returned to the House, the Speaker and several members of Congress called for a revote due to the circumstances. On the second vote, the amendment failed. With the help of her colleagues, Patsy Mink had preserved Title IX.

In 1975, Patsy left the House of Representatives to run for Senate. She lost. But she remained committed to public service, working in various city, state, and national offices before returning to the House of Representatives, completing a term for a successor. Six weeks later, she was elected to a full term and went on to be reelected six more times.

Patsy Mink died a week after she won the 2002 primary election. She was posthumously reelected to Congress. In 2002, Congress renamed Title IX the Patsy T. Mink Equal Opportunity in Education Act.

Supreme Court Justice **Ruth Bader Ginsburg (1933–2020)** wrote arguments and opinions to fight for women's equality. As cofounder and head of the Women's Rights Project at the ACLU, she brought six equal-rights cases before the Supreme Court. Because of her work, the Supreme Court decided that the Fourteenth Amendment's Equal Protection Clause also applies to women.

WRITE TO KNOW

Anyone can write legislation to address a problem. Ideas are usually written in the form of bills and presented by a member of Congress.

WRITE NOW

What if you took your biggest worries and created legislation to improve people's lives? Make a list of your worries. Imagine creative ideas for solving these problems. Research, write, and polish these ideas for legislation—and send them to your representative.

Anne Frank

Diarist, 1929–1945

Write to Express:
The Diary of Anne Frank

On her thirteenth birthday, Anne Frank discovered a pile of presents on the dining room table. She was delighted to find a diary covered in a red and light green plaid cloth. Later that day, she wrote:

> *I hope I will be able to confide everything to you, as I have never been able to confide in anyone, and I hope you will be a great source of comfort and support.*

Anne needed a friend more than ever. As a young Jewish girl growing up in Amsterdam during World War II, she couldn't attend the movies or visit the park with her friends. In 1942, the Nazis began deporting Jewish people to death camps in Poland. The Frank family hid in a small, secret apartment called the Secret Annex above Anne's father's office.

Anne's diary became her best friend. She wrote her entries as letters, mostly to Kitty Francken, a character in her favorite books. She also wrote stories and fairy tales and started a novel. Anne began revising her diary, hoping to publish a book based on it after the war. Writing helped Anne understand her feelings and gave her a place to think about what was happening both in the annex and in the world. Writing also kept Anne hopeful:

> *When I write I can shake off all my cares. My sorrow disappears, my spirits are revived! But, and that's a great big question, will I ever be able to write something great, will I ever become a journalist or a writer?*

The Frank family lived in the annex for 761 days. Three days after Anne wrote her last diary entry, the Nazi police raided the annex and captured everyone. Miep Gies, one of the women who had been protecting the family, collected all of Anne's writing and locked it in her desk.

The whole family was deported to the concentration camp at Auschwitz-Birkenau. Anne and her sister Margot were later sent to another camp, Bergen-Belsen. Both sisters became ill with typhus and died within days of each other. Anne's father, Otto Frank, was the only person from the annex to survive.

Rywka Lipszyc (1929–1945) wrote her diary while living in the Lodz Ghetto, a small Jewish community segregated by the Nazis. Like Anne, she was sent to Auschwitz-Birkenau in 1944, and her notebook was found there. Known as *Rywka's Diary: The Writings of a Jewish Girl from the Lodz Ghetto*, it reveals that Rywka felt as strongly as Anne did about writing: "Oh, to write! . . . To be able to write, to make pen move on paper! I need to write."

After the war, Miep gave Otto all of Anne's writing: her plaid diary, several notebooks, and 327 loose sheets of thin paper.

Otto Frank published Anne's diaries in March 1947 as *The House Behind*. The first American edition appeared in 1952 as *Anne Frank: The Diary of a Young Girl*. Anne's diary has been translated into seventy languages and has sold more than thirty million copies worldwide.

When she was ten years old, **Zlata Filipović (1980–)** began writing about how the Bosnian war restricted her life. In 1992, *Zlata's Diary: A Child's Life in Wartime Sarajevo* was published. A year later, the United Nations helped her and her mother escape to Paris. Inspired by Anne Frank's diary, "Kitty," she named hers Mimmy: "My diary became more than a place to record daily events. It became a friend."

WRITE TO KNOW

In addition to keeping a diary, Anne Frank collected favorite quotes in a separate journal, which she called her "book of beautiful sentences." Many people use journals to document their experiences and play with ideas. Here are a few journal types:

ART: Frida Kahlo (1907–1954) combined sketches, watercolor paintings, and writing to reflect on her life.

BULLET: Developed by Ryder Carroll (1981–) to cope with a learning disability, users track habits, log events, and plan projects.

DREAM: Author Jack Kerouac (1922–1969) recorded and analyzed his dreams in a notebook, which inspired his novel *Book of Dreams*.

SPIRITUAL: Bruce Lee (1940–1973), famous for his martial arts films, kept journals filled with poetry, affirmations, and philosophical reflections. A spiritual journal may also include prayers and quotes.

TRAVEL: Meriwether Lewis (1774–1809) and William Clark (1770–1838) wrote eighteen journals chronicling their more than 8,000-mile journey from the Midwest to the West Coast.

WRITE NOW

Create your own journal using a spiral notebook, a composition book, or loose paper. Decorate the cover with doodles, stickers, washi tape, or whatever else you find. Fill your journal with your thoughts and feelings, poems, sketches, designs, or inventions.

The nicest part is being able to write down all my thoughts and feelings; otherwise, I'd absolutely suffocate.

—*Anne Frank*

The Rev. Dr. Martin Luther King Jr.

Minister and Activist, 1929–1968

Write to Persuade:

"Letter from a Birmingham Jail"

The Rev. Dr. Martin Luther King Jr. changed the world through his words and actions:

> *We adopt the means of nonviolence because our end is a community at peace with itself. We will try to persuade with our words, but if our words fail, we will try to persuade with our acts.*

Martin wanted to use principles of nonviolent action to end racial segregation in Birmingham, Alabama. The city's laws made it illegal for Black and white people to dine, shop, or even play sports together. Black people endured injustice in the courts, racially motivated bombings, and other violent attacks.

Martin worked with other Christian leaders to boycott the downtown shops. On Good Friday, April 12, 1963, Martin and fellow minister Ralph Abernathy led a march in Birmingham. Because the state had issued an injunction against public protests, the men were arrested and jailed. Martin was placed in solitary confinement.

Journalist **Ethel Lois Payne (1911–1991)** wrote about the civil rights movement for the *Chicago Defender*, interviewing Martin Luther King Jr. before he became famous. The first Black woman to join the White House Press Corps, Ethel covered seven presidents. In 1970, she became the first Black woman to serve as a radio and television commentator on a national network (CBS).

A friend smuggled in a newspaper containing a letter from eight religious leaders, titled "An Appeal for Law and Order and Common Sense." The clergy urged Martin and his colleagues to obey the law, stop demonstrating, and take the battle for civil rights to the courts.

Never before have I written so long a letter. I'm afraid it is much too long to take your precious time. I can assure you that it would have been much shorter if I had been writing from a comfortable desk, but what else can one do when he is alone in a narrow jail cell, other than write long letters, think long thoughts and pray long prayers?

—*The Rev. Dr. Martin Luther King Jr.*

Martin wanted to address their concerns because the rights and lives of so many people were at stake. He wrote a letter to the leaders, scribbling notes in the margins of the newspaper. When he'd covered every blank surface, he wrote on the prison's rough toilet paper. Martin had no books, so he quoted from memory.

In his letter, Martin addressed each of the clergy's points. They criticized outsiders for interfering in a local fight. Martin said that just like the apostle Paul from the Bible, he was called to carry the gospel beyond his own home:

> *Injustice anywhere is a threat to justice everywhere. We are caught in an inescapable network of mutuality, tied in a single garment of destiny. Whatever affects one directly, affects all indirectly.*

The clergy criticized leaders for breaking the law. Martin quoted the Christian theologian Augustine: "An unjust law is no law at all." He reminded them that everything Hitler did in Germany was legal, and anyone who aided Jewish people broke the law.

The clergy had accused Black leaders of being extremists. Martin claimed the label, saying, "I gradually gained a measure of satisfaction from the label. Was not Jesus an extremist for love?"

During his eight-day stay in the Birmingham jail, Martin's lawyers snuck out pieces of his writings. Supporters typed up and assembled those excerpts into the seven-thousand-word finished letter. The Sunday after he was released from jail, the Rev. Dr. Martin Luther King Jr. preached a version of

the letter at the Sixteenth Street Baptist Church in Birmingham.

In June 1963, the whole letter was published for the first time in *Liberation* magazine. Martin's letter brought his argument for nonviolent resistance to racism to a national stage.

When Martin Luther King Jr. received the Nobel Peace Prize in 1964, the letter reached a global audience. Martin's letter helped pave the way for people to fight for justice all over the world.

Civil rights organizer **Bayard Rustin (1912–1987)** taught King about nonviolence, coordinated the Freedom Rides, and helped set up the March on Washington for Jobs and Freedom. Bayard coined the phrase "speak truth to power" and wrote *Speak Truth to Power: A Quaker Search for an Alternative to Violence*. In the 1980s, he publicly advocated for gay rights.

WRITE TO KNOW

In his letter, Martin Luther King Jr. used these tools to write to persuade:

CREDIBILITY: Show people they can trust you and your expertise.

REASON: Provide research, statistics, or other evidence.

EMOTION: Use stories and images to appeal to emotions.

WRITE NOW

Write a statement or letter to persuade readers to make changes they think are too big or too scary to try.

Audre Lorde

Poet, Feminist, and Activist,
1934–1992

Write to Voice: "Power"

Audre Lorde didn't speak until she was four. She screamed. Told she was too young to attend the library's story hour with her sisters, she threw a tantrum: "I lay spread-eagled on the floor . . . like a furious little brown toad, screaming bloody murder."

A librarian offered to read her a story. Audre would later say that deed saved her life. "Books were where I found sustenance, and from telling myself stories at night to writing them down was a very short space."

> When I dare to be powerful, to use my strength in the service of my vision, then it becomes less and less important whether I am afraid.
>
> —*Audre Lorde*

The youngest daughter of Caribbean immigrants, Audre believed she was at war with her parents and sisters: "I was a very difficult child. I was a rebel from the time I can remember. . . . It was their camp against mine." She struggled to fit in with other children and had difficulty sharing her feelings. She communicated through poetry:

> *People would say, well, what do you think, Audre? What happened to you yesterday? And I would recite a poem and somewhere in that poem there would be a line or a feeling I would be sharing.*

In high school, Audre worked on the school newspaper and took poetry classes from the Harlem Writers Guild. When she was fifteen years old, she had her first poem published in *Seventeen* magazine.

Audre described herself as thinking in poems. One morning while studying at the National University of Mexico, she was struck by the quality of light and its connection to words. She wanted her poetry to recreate that feeling for readers.

Audre's first book of poetry, *The First Cities*, was published in 1968. Exhausted from working as a librarian, writing poetry, and raising her children, she spent six weeks as the writer in residence at Tougaloo College in Mississippi. Leading writing workshops with young people ignited a new passion: teaching. She also fell in love with a woman, Frances Clayton, a psychology professor who taught at the college.

Audre returned to New York and ended her marriage. She began a teaching career that would span multiple universities and two countries over the next twenty-some years. Audre and Frances moved to a big house on Staten Island, where they raised Audre's children together.

When Audre heard that a police officer had been acquitted for shooting an unarmed ten-year-old boy in the back, she wrote a poem in response. "Power" tells the story of Clifford Glover's death—the terror and loneliness of his last moments.

Novelist **Toni Morrison (1931–2019)** and Audre Lorde share their birthday, February 18. As one of the first Black female editors in publishing, Toni championed the voices of Black authors. But Toni is best known for writing novels like *The Bluest Eye* and *Beloved.* In 1993, Toni Morrison was awarded the Nobel Prize for Literature, becoming the first Black woman to win a Nobel Prize.

Audre wrote poetry for the girl she once was, the child who was afraid to tell her truth. She wrote poetry to protest injustice. She wrote to help other people tell their stories:

Primarily, I write for those women who do not speak; who do not have verbalization because they, we, are so terrified, because we are taught to respect fear more than ourselves. We've been taught to respect our fears, but we must learn to respect ourselves and our needs.

What would you write about if you were not afraid? Write it!

WRITE TO CREATE

The lawyer Kimberlé Crenshaw coined the term *intersectionality* in 1989. Years earlier, Audre Lorde fought against being limited to a single identity and introduced herself as a "black, lesbian, mother, warrior, poet." She advocated for people to define and embrace their multiple identities, saying, "Only by learning to live in harmony with your contradictions can you keep it all afloat."

Create a mind map of you and your identities. Consider the names you answer to, the titles or terms you identify with (sister, son, athlete, artist), the groups you belong to, and the people you love. Add your hopes, wishes, beliefs, and more. Then claim your identities in a statement.

Poet, novelist, and playwright **Ntozake Shange (1948–2018)** wrote many successful plays, including *For Colored Girls Who Have Considered Suicide/When the Rainbow Is Enuf*. In the twenty-part choreopoem, Ntozake combined poetry, dance, and music to tell the stories of women of color in the United States. The play was later adapted into both a book and a movie.

Octavia Butler

Science Fiction Author,
1947–2006

Write to Persist:
Patternmaster

As a child, Octavia Butler wrote stories "to escape loneliness and boredom."

Before Octavia was born, her four older brothers died as infants. Her father died when she was young. Classmates bullied Octavia, who was tall for her age and socially anxious:

> *I was quiet, bookish, and in spite of my size, hopeless at sports. In short, I was different. And even in the earliest grades, I got pounded for it.*

Despite being mildly dyslexic, Octavia learned to read before she started school. She entertained herself by making up stories. When she realized she was forgetting some of her earlier stories, she wrote them down. Octavia loved reading about science and dreamed of traveling to the places she read about in *National Geographic*. But she also liked to use her imagination:

> *I fantasized living impossible, but interesting lives—magical lives in which I could fly like Superman, communicate with animals, control people's minds. I became a magical horse on an island of horses.*

When she was twelve, Octavia watched the science fiction movie *Devil Girl from Mars* and thought, "Geez, I can write a better story than that!" and "Somebody got *paid* for writing that story!" She began writing science fiction.

Octavia didn't have much support for her dream. Her mother wanted her to be a secretary and her aunt hoped she'd study nursing, saying: "Negroes can't be writers." A professor told her not to use Black characters in her stories unless their Blackness was essential to the plot. But Octavia had a different vision:

> *When I began writing science fiction, when I began reading, heck, I wasn't in any of this stuff I read. . . . I certainly wasn't in the science fiction. The only black people you found were occasional characters or characters who were so feeble-witted that they couldn't manage anything, anyway. I wrote myself in, since I'm me and I'm here and I'm writing. I can write my own stories and I can write myself in.*

After graduating with an associate's degree, Octavia worked as a warehouse worker, dishwasher, potato chip inspector, and telemarketer. She got up every day at 2 a.m. to write and then went to work.

Octavia also took writing classes from the University of California–Los Angeles extension program. In 1969, she met science

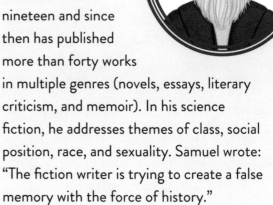

Samuel Delany (1942–) wrote his first novel at nineteen and since then has published more than forty works in multiple genres (novels, essays, literary criticism, and memoir). In his science fiction, he addresses themes of class, social position, race, and sexuality. Samuel wrote: "The fiction writer is trying to create a false memory with the force of history."

fiction writer Harlan Ellison, who had written for *Star Trek*. He encouraged her to attend a national workshop for science fiction writers, where she sold her first two stories.

In December 1975, Octavia sold her first novel to Doubleday publishing company. She'd been creating the world and the characters for *Patternmaster* since she was a little girl:

> *I carried a big notebook around so that whenever I had some time I could write in it. That way, I didn't have to be lonely. I usually had very few friends, and I was lonely. But when I wrote I wasn't.*

Octavia went on to write more than fifteen books. In 2000, she received a PEN award for lifetime achievement.

My most important talent—or habit—was persistence. Without it, I would have given up writing long before I finished my first novel. It's amazing what we can do if we simply refuse to give up.

—*Octavia Butler*

WRITE TO KNOW

Octavia Butler had this note posted by her desk: "Tell stories filled with facts. Make people touch and taste and know. Make people FEEL! FEEL! FEEL!" Sensory details help your readers feel what your characters are experiencing. What words or actions might help people see that a character feels a certain emotion?

WRITE NOW

Science fiction authors ask, "What would happen if . . . ?" and follow their questions to a story idea. Set a timer for ten minutes, come up with a "What if . . . ?" question, and brainstorm answers to it. Use one of your answers to write a story.

Science fiction author **N. K. Jemisin (1972–)** began writing stories when she was eight. Because she didn't see many Black science fiction writers, she worried she wouldn't be successful. In 2018, she became the first person to win three consecutive Hugo awards for best novel. N. K. explores race and ecology in her fiction. She wrote: "I just want to write about things blowing up. Gods and planets and moons crashing into things. But what I write ends up being very political."

Sandra Cisneros

Novelist and Poet, 1954–

Write to Name:
*The House
on Mango Street*

Sandra Cisneros's father often introduced himself by saying, "I have seven sons." Although he meant seven children, the slip left Sandra feeling invisible. Her six brothers paired up to play, leaving her alone.

> *But that aloneness, that loneliness, was good for a would-be writer—it allowed me time to think and think, to imagine, to read and prepare myself.*

Sandra grew up in Chicago, near her mother's extended Mexican American family. When her father felt nostalgic, the family packed up everything and moved to her grandparents' house in Mexico City, returning to Chicago every time.

In fifth grade, Sandra's teacher called her mother to talk about Sandra's daydreaming. That year she earned only Cs and Ds. Sandra later reflected:

> *Too bad there was no grade for art, or I would've gotten an A. Too bad there was no credit for the seven or eight books I borrowed every week from the public library. . . . I have always been a daydreamer, and that's a lucky thing for a writer. Because what is a daydreamer if not another word for thinker, visionary, intuitive—all wonderful words synonymous with "girl."*

Sandra's mother was a voracious reader who gave her daughter time to read and study. Sandra wrote her first poem at ten. In high school, she wrote poetry and edited the school literary magazine, becoming known as "the poet."

At first, Sandra imitated the voices of male poets. In graduate school, Sandra realized she had her own stories to tell. Inspired by the voices of the people in her culture, she wrote poems about experiences of

When **S. E. Hinton (1948–)** was sixteen, she couldn't find a novel that captured her experience with two rival gangs at her school, so she wrote *The Outsiders*. The book has sold more than fourteen million copies.

the "silent women." Sandra described herself as "always straddling two countries . . . but not belonging to either culture." This divided life gave her a purpose:

> *I'm a translator. I'm an amphibian. I can travel in both worlds. What I'm saying is very important for the Latino community, but it is also important for the white community to hear.*

Sandra has supported herself by taking on many jobs, including high school and college teacher, administrative assistant, college recruiter, counselor, poet in the schools, and arts administrator. She chose to not marry or have children, finding writing to be her best partner. Sandra says that all she needs to write is her house, a writing machine, and her beloved pets.

Gloria Anzaldúa (1942–2004) was a poet who identified as Chicana (Mexican American) and queer. The child of migrant farmers, she grew up on the Texas-Mexico border. In her best-known work, *Borderlands/La Frontera: The New Mestiza*, she used variations of both English and Spanish to demonstrate what living on the border felt like.

Sandra reflected on the dream of having a house of her own in the novel *The House on Mango Street*, where the teenage writer Esperanza dreams of "a space for myself to go, clean as paper before the poem." Published in 1984 when Sandra was just twenty-nine years old, *The House on Mango Street* has sold over six million copies and has been translated into more than twenty languages.

> I don't think about tone or imitating text when I write. I just write in my own true voice, the one that is mine and not anyone else's.
>
> —*Sandra Cisneros*

WRITE TO KNOW

How short is a short story? According to a popular (and probably untrue) anecdote, Ernest Hemingway bet his friends that he could write a six-word novel. He scribbled on a napkin: "For sale: baby shoes, never worn." In 2006, *Smith* magazine asked readers to share their life stories in just six words. The magazine received one thousand submissions and published them into several books.

WRITE NOW

In *The House on Mango Street*, the character Esperanza tells the reader about the origin of her name. Write a six-word memoir or a short story about where your name comes from, what it means, and how it does or does not reflect who you are.

Joy Harjo (1951–) is a musician, poet, and playwright. She's a member of the Muscogee (Creek) Nation and draws on the symbols, imagery, and stories from her heritage in her writing. In 2019, Joy was named the first Native American US Poet Laureate. Sandra and Joy became friends at graduate school and support each other's work.

Write to Illustrate:
Comic Books and Graphic Novels

A picture is worth a thousand words.

Humans have been proving that adage for eons. Thirty thousand years ago, artists in Africa drew, painted, and engraved scenes from daily life on rocks. Since then, people have engraved stories on stone columns and embroidered them into tapestries. But you can't curl up with a cave wall. Unless you lived near these artifacts, you'd have to take a road trip to read their stories.

The printing press changed that, making it possible to produce and distribute broadsheets—a single large piece of paper printed with words and images. Artists sketched and sold these at public executions, which attracted as many as 100,000 people.

Printers thought readers might like funny stories too, and created satirical broadsheets. These depicted funny caricatures of famous people. Artists had to be careful—royal rulers were a bit touchy about how people portrayed them. Cartoonists sometimes got imprisoned or even put to death for their work.

Jackie Ormes (1911–1985) was the first published female Black American cartoonist. She created *Torchy Brown in Dixie to Harlem*, which followed a teen performer on his journey to fame at the Cotton Club. Jackie also created the *Patty-Jo 'n' Ginger* single-panel cartoon and transformed her character Patty-Jo into the first realistic Black doll for little girls.

Technology improved. Printers discovered how to reproduce art and cheaply bind multiple sheets together. They published "penny dreadfuls"—magazines filled with illustrated stories for both adults and children. The first genuine comic strip magazine that featured a continuing character was *Ally Sloper's Half Holiday* (1884).

In the United States, newspapers made comics popular. In 1933, a publisher compiled newspaper funnies and released the first comic book: *Famous Funnies: A Carnival of Comics*. At ten cents, the comic book was considered pricey, but it sold over 180,000 copies.

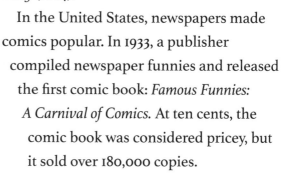

In 1935, National Allied Publications (now DC Comics) released the first comic book with original material. *New Fun Comics* debuted characters that readers would come to adore: Doctor Fate, The Spectre, Green Arrow, Aquaman, and Superboy. This was quickly followed by comic books featuring Superman and Batman.

Timely (now Marvel) began producing Marvel Mystery Comics in the 1930s and introduced its own roster of superheroes, including the Human Torch, the Sub-Mariner, and the Masked Raider. In the 1940s, Marvel introduced Captain America, who remains a popular character today. Comic books quickly gained popularity during the 1940s and '50s. Writers created some of comics' most beloved characters, including the Flash, Green Lantern, Hulk, and Spider-Man.

In the mid-1950s, the popular psychiatrist Fredric Wertham announced that reading comic books led to juvenile delinquency. Stories about the dangers of comic books popped up on television and in popular magazines. Parents worried about their children, and some ordered them to toss or burn their comic books.

As a result, the Comic Magazine Association of America formed the Comics Code Authority (now defunct) to review comic books. If the

Stan Lee (1922–2018) began working at Timely Comics as a teenager, refilling ink and writing filler. He co-created beloved superheroes including Spider-Man, Black Panther, the Hulk, and the Fantastic Four. Stan became the creative leader of Marvel, and helped transform the industry by insisting on crafting comic book heroes with human qualities, including flaws, self-doubts, and passions for people and issues.

> **Those stories have room for everyone, regardless of their race, gender, religion, or color of their skin. The only things we don't have room for are hatred, intolerance, and bigotry.**
>
> —*Stan Lee*

committee approved of the content, they would provide their Seal of Approval. Any comic book that contained crime or dark fantasy was either canceled or cleaned up.

MAD magazine avoided review by changing its format from a comic book to a magazine. Other comic book creators made underground "comix" to write stories about issues that mattered to them, including feminism, civil rights, LGBT rights, and the Vietnam War. Later researchers found that Dr. Wertham was wrong: he had twisted the research and overstated his case to gain popularity.

For years, readers could only buy comic books by subscribing or stopping at a newsstand. In the 1970s, small comic-book stores began sprouting up. Readers could get the new issues as well as all of the back issues.

As comic books steamed forward, a new genre hit the scene: graphic novels. In 1964, a fan historian used the term *graphic novel* in an article. The term didn't become mainstream until the publication of Art Spiegelman's Pulitzer Prize–winning graphic novel *Maus* (1986), which told the true story of his parents' experience during the Holocaust.

Since then, graphic novels have exploded in popularity and have become recognized as a respected literary form. They've won nearly every literary award. And in a delicious irony, the form once decried for ruining children is now regularly used in the classroom. Thankfully, that doesn't make graphic novels any less fun to read.

Gene Luen Yang

Cartoonist and Graphic Novelist,
1973–

Write to Picture:
American Born Chinese

Gene Luen Yang grew up surrounded by storytelling. His parents were immigrants and told stories to teach him about their cultures. Gene began drawing when he was two, and wanted to be an animator for Disney.

Though he was a slow reader, Gene loved books. In fifth grade, Gene's mother bought him his first comic book:

> *I stayed up nights thinking about Superman, the Atomic Knights, mutated dogs, and comic books; about how this combination of words and pictures did something in my head that had never happened before.*

Gene wanted more stories and regularly visited the local comic shop. He and a good friend created their own comic books. They developed the stories together, then Gene would sketch the comics, and his friend would ink them. They sold copies to their friends for fifty cents each.

Classmates regularly teased Gene, one of the few Asian American students at his school. By high school, he had a group of friends he connected with over mahjong, comic books, and running cross-country.

Gene wanted to major in art at college. His father insisted he try something more practical. He majored in computer science and minored in creative writing. After college he worked for a time as a computer engineer, then left to teach high school.

As a teacher, Gene worked as a long-term math sub. When classes conflicted with his other duties, he made video lectures, thinking, "Kids love screens, right?" The students told Gene he was even more boring on video than in person. So he tried a new approach: creating a comic strip for each lesson. It worked. The students loved learning from the comics.

When Gene wrote *American Born Chinese*, he placed the early chapters online. He also created mini-comics—hand-printed, photocopied comics he'd give to family members or sell at comic conventions.

American Born Chinese has sold over 500,000 copies and is taught in high school and college classrooms across the country. It was the first graphic novel to win the Michael L. Printz Award from the American Library Association, which recognizes the best books for teens.

Jerry Craft (1963–) chronicled the challenge of moving between two different worlds and not fitting in anywhere in *New Kid*, the first graphic novel to win the Newbery Award. He's also one of the few Black American cartoonists to have a syndicated comic strip, *Mama's Boyz* (1995–2013).

Gene admits to struggling with self-doubt and fear, especially when he tries new things. He's learned to push through the fear and find the happy ending:

> *With every project I've ever done, I've felt like quitting when I was three-fourths of the way done. Some other shiny new idea will pop up in my head, and I'll want to move on. It took me a long time to realize that feeling is normal, and that it goes away if I can just push to the finish line.*

WRITE NOW

In *American Born Chinese*, Gene Luen Yang wove together three stories—a Chinese American boy trying to fit in at his new school, an American boy embarrassed by the visit of his Chinese cousin, and the traditional legend of "the Monkey King." Write a story about trying to fit in or being embarrassed. Use a legend to help explain your experience.

When **Cece Bell (1970–)** was growing up, she wished hearing people could understand what it was like to be deaf and carry around the Phonic Ear to hear. She wrote about her experiences in the graphic novel *El Deafo*, a Newbery Honor book and winner of the Eisner medal.

Get in the habit of creation. The habit is almost more important than the work itself. I tell students who are interested in making anything creative to set up a time regularly to work on their creative work, and to make sure to think of that time as sacred, to keep it sacred.

—*Gene Luen Yang*

WRITE TO CREATE

How would you tell your story in graphic form? Write a script for your story, describing visual images. Use a storyboard to sketch out a rough plan of how you will lay out the story. Now you're ready to begin creating the final product!

In sixth grade, **Raina Telgemeier (1977–)** fell and knocked out her two front teeth, and then wrote about it in her graphic memoir *Smile*, which won the Eisner medal. In *Guts*, Raina wrote about dealing with the stomach problems that come with her anxiety.

Sonita Alizadeh

Rapper and Activist,
1996–

Write to Rebel:
"Brides for Sale"

When Sonita was just ten, her parents tried to sell her as a bride. The deal fell through.

Born in Afghanistan during the Taliban regime, Sonita couldn't watch movies, play a musical instrument, or go online because the Taliban had banned these activities. Suicide bombings and roadside attacks happened regularly. To escape, Sonita's family walked hundreds of miles through rain and snow to Iran. There, they lived as undocumented refugees. Because she didn't have papers, she couldn't attend public school. She cleaned offices and sold handicrafts on the street to earn money for her family.

Sonita attended classes at a nonprofit for Afghan refugees and learned to read and write. She loved writing poetry and making art. Sonita explored writing music, but she didn't feel like her lyrics fit into pop songs. One night while she was cleaning an office, she heard Eminem on the radio and fell in love with rap music. She said,

Of all the genres, rap made me feel good. It was amazing to me how we combine powerful words and phrases, all delivered in a melodic and rhyming way that captivates the soul and hearts of the listener.

Between jobs and classes, Sonita wrote and practiced her music, hiding her lyrics in her backpack. Rebelling against an Iranian law prohibiting women from singing, she recorded songs about Afghan politics, child labor, and being a refugee.

Sonita's mother announced that they planned to sell Sonita into marriage with an older man for $9,000. The money would help buy her brother's bride. But then a documentary filmmaker offered to pay Sonita's mother $2,000 to purchase six months of freedom for the teen.

Sonita and the filmmaker made her music video "Brides for Sale." In the video, Sonita rapped: "But I wish you go over Quran. I wish you understand that it never said women are for sale." The video went viral, and a nonprofit organization in the United States helped Sonita leave Iran to finish her education and pursue a music career.

Sonita now advocates for girls' and women's rights, primarily fighting to end child marriage. When she was in the program for Afghan refugees, classmates as young as twelve years old would suddenly disappear from school because they were preparing to get married. These girls

The band **Bikini Kill (formed in 1990)** wrote the song "Rebel Girl," which became an anthem for the Riot Grrrl movement. This movement combined feminism, punk style, and anti-oppression politics in music and zines. It addressed issues such as racism, sexism, and sexual abuse.

> Rap, music, and poetry have been outlets for me to express myself to the world. They let me tell my story. They're platforms to share the words that are in my heart.

—*Sonita Alizadeh*

lose their education and the possibility of earning an income. Many child brides are beaten by their husbands.

Sonita has won many awards for her work to end child marriage and for "using rap music to empower the girls of Afghanistan." As a musician and an activist, she calls herself a "raptivist."

As high school students in Burlington, Vermont, **Kiran Waqar, Hawa Adam, Lena Ginawi, and Balkisa Abdikadir** formed a youth slam poetry group called Muslim Girls Making Change (MGMC) to change the conversation about young people, immigration, and being Muslim in America. They use their poetry and activism to support initiatives for change.

WRITE TO KNOW

For centuries, people have written protest songs to speak against injustice. Protestors borrow popular tunes, or create their own, and craft words that promote their cause.

- "Go Down, Moses" tells the story of the people of Israel being freed from slavery in Egypt. Harriet Tubman sang this song on the Underground Railroad to warn people to stay hidden because danger was coming.

- A Black preacher, the Rev. Charles Abbot Tindley, wrote the words for "I Shall Overcome Someday" and set it to a nineteenth century spiritual. Protestors changed the words to "We Shall Overcome" and sang it to demand justice during the 1940s labor protests, the 1960s civil rights movement, and Black Lives Matter protests.

> Raised in Michigan, rapper and chaplain **Mona Haydar (1988–)** began performing spoken word poetry at age fourteen. Her debut single, "Hijabi (Wrap My Hijab)," encourages listeners to love women as they are. The song went viral, and Billboard named it one of the "20 Best Protest Songs of 2017."

- What's your favorite protest song?

WRITE NOW

Sonita Alizadeh's protest song started with a very personal problem. Think of a cause that affects you or people you love, and write a protest song about it.

WRITE TO CREATE

Sonita created a "dream book," filled with pictures and words about her future life. This book inspired many of her songs. Make your own dream book.

Malala Yousafzai

Activist, 1997–

Write to Advocate:
I Am Malala

Malala grew up in a large city in Pakistan. Her father ran a small school, and they lived in the apartment above it. As a toddler, Malala wandered into classrooms and imitated the teacher.

In grade school, Malala entered a speech competition. Following tradition, her father wrote her speech. Even though she was at the top of her class, Malala trembled and rushed through the words. She realized,

> *Sometimes it's better to tell your own story. I started writing my own speeches and changing the way I delivered them, from my heart rather than from a sheet of paper.*

In the fall of 2007, the Taliban took control of her district. They banned watching television, listening to music, and dancing. They blew up or burned down more than one hundred schools in Malala's community.

In January 2009, they issued an edict banning girls from attending school.

Malala and her father fought to keep her school open. Malala spoke about her mission: "How dare the Taliban take away my basic right to education?" Malala did not back down and later said, "We were scared, but our fear was not as strong as our courage."

A reporter from the BBC radio called Malala's family, looking for a female student or teacher to write a blog. Several girls refused, saying it would be too dangerous. Malala leapt at the chance, writing under a pseudonym. Her first post was about the fear she experienced going to school.

Shortly after the blog launched, Malala's school closed. Her family fled their home. When Malala was revealed as the blogger for the BBC, she became even more outspoken.

In 2011, Malala received Pakistan's first-ever National Peace Prize. The Taliban issued death threats against her. One day, as she was on the way home from school, two men stopped her bus, and one of them shot Malala in the head. Two of her friends were also injured.

Malala underwent several surgeries and extensive rehabilitation. During this time, she realized something: "I knew I had a choice: I could live a quiet life or I could make the most of this new life I had been given. I determined to continue my fight until every girl could go to school."

With the help of her father, Malala set up the Malala Fund to give all girls the opportunity to achieve the future they choose. In 2014, Malala became the youngest person to receive the Nobel Peace Prize. Since then, she has written several books, graduated from Oxford University, and continues to work for peace. She implores world leaders to "choose books over bullets."

When she was eleven years old, **Tuba Sahaab (1997–)** fought against the Taliban, who banned girls from school and burned their books. Tuba wrote poetry to support the education of girls, feeding and clothing the poor, and creating a peaceful world. She shared her poetry with newspapers and the radio in Pakistan.

WRITE TO KNOW

When Malala blogged, her editor encouraged her to write about her personal feelings, construct "pungent sentences," and share personal details about her family's life. Here are more blogging tips:

DEVELOP CONTENT

- Find a niche that reflects your passion, experience, and expertise.
- Write in your voice and tell your stories.

DESIGN YOUR BLOG

- Create a simple design with clear navigation tools.
- Make it visual, using headers, photos, and graphics.

ATTRACT READERS

- Publish regularly on topics that engage your ideal reader.
- Interact with readers through comments and social media.

WRITE NOW

Kids blog about everything from overcoming social anxiety to confronting racism. If you could advocate for something on a blog, what would you write about? Journal about your idea, and then plan your blog.

When eleven-year-old **Marley Dias (2005–)** set out to collect one thousand books featuring interesting Black girls, she created the hashtag #1000blackgirlbooks. The tweet worked, and Marley has donated thousands of books to schools and libraries. She even wrote a book about her work, *Marley Dias Gets It Done: And So Can You!*

WRITE TO CREATE

Malala uses the hashtag #booksnotbullets. She wrote, "Books not bullets is not an empty slogan, it is a strategy to build lasting peace and tackle the huge challenges facing our world." What hashtag could you use with your blog? How else could you use a slogan?

I began to see that the pen and the words that come from it can be much more powerful than machine guns, tanks or helicopters. We were learning how to struggle. And we were learning how powerful we are when we speak.

—*Malala Yousafzai*

Sophie Cruz

Activist, 2010–

Write to Request:
Letter to Pope Francis

Sophie Cruz took dance lessons and recited poetry. She learned karate so she could defend herself. When she asked to visit her grandfather in Mexico, her parents refused. Sophie didn't understand why. Her parents explained that they couldn't go because they didn't have the papers necessary to come back into the United States. Sophie said, "Let's fight for a green card."

An advocacy group saw Sophie perform a Mexican folk dance and admired her eloquence. They invited Sophie to come to Washington, DC, for the pope's visit. Sophie brought with her a letter she'd written for the pope.

Standing with her father outside the White House, Sophie tried to hand her letter to the pope. Security stopped her. But Sophie didn't give up. At another point in the parade route, her dad lifted her over the barrier, and she ran toward the pope. Once again, security moved to stop her. The pope intervened—asking security to bring Sophie to him. The two hugged. Sophie delivered her letter, and the pope blessed her. When a reporter asked her how she had the courage to approach the pope, she said, "God made me like that."

In her letter, Sophie told the pope that she was sad and afraid that US Immigration and Customs Enforcement would deport her parents. She argued for her right to be happy and to be raised by her parents. She wrote about her father's hard work and how immigrants like her dad "feed this country." She ended the letter with a plea for herself and other children:

> *Don't forget about us the children, or about those who suffer because they're not with their parents because of war, because of violence, because of hunger.*

The letter included a picture she had drawn, with the pope in the center, holding hands with Sophie and her friends. The words said: "My friends and I love each other no matter our skin color." Within hours, Sophie's encounter with Pope Francis became big news. When the pope spoke before a joint session of Congress, he advocated for the rights of refugees and immigrants.

Later, President Obama invited Sophie to the White House to celebrate Cinco de Mayo with him. Because of her parents' immigration status, they could not go with her. At the Women's March on Washington in 2017, Sophie Cruz spoke eloquently in Spanish and English, declaring: "Let us fight with love, faith, and courage so that our families will not be destroyed."

Sophie hasn't stopped writing. In 2017, she and other children of undocumented immigrants wrote Presidents' Day letters to President Donald Trump. Sophie wrote, "Greatness is what we do for others, not who we are." She asked the president to follow in the legacy of the office, working for "equality, justice, respect, peace."

WRITE TO KNOW

A letter-writing campaign can be an effective tool for asking lawmakers, officials, and corporations to make changes.

1. Choose the issue and articulate what you want.
2. Identify individuals and organizations who have power to make changes.

> **We are here together making a chain of love to protect our families. . . . I also want to tell the children not to be afraid, because we are not alone.**
>
> —*Sophie Cruz*

From the time **Amariyanna "Mari" Copeny (2007–)** was eight years old, she knew that using her home's water could be dangerous. She took a bus to Washington, DC, to attend a congressional hearing on the water crisis in her hometown of Flint, Michigan. On her way, Mari wrote a letter to President Barack Obama, asking him to visit Flint. He wrote back, saying: "Letters from kids like you are what make me so optimistic for the future." President Obama visited Flint on May 4, 2016, bringing national attention to the town's water crisis. Since then, Mari has raised more than $500,000 for her community and is working to provide residents across the country with safe water filters.

3. Create a prototype of the letter, including:
   - A clear demand: What do you want the recipient to do?
   - A short list of reasons or evidence supporting your demand.
   - Suggestions for how letter writers can personalize their letters, perhaps by sharing how the issue affects their lives.

WRITE NOW

What do you need to ask for? Who would you like to thank? What issue matters to you? Write a letter to a caregiver, teacher, or lawmaker, expressing your hopes and feelings.

Write to Change:
Speeches at March for Our Lives

When people talk about events like the Holocaust or school shootings, they sometimes ask, "What would you do?" In horrible situations like these, would you have risked your life to save someone else? Would you speak out against injustice? Or would you stay silent?

The students of Marjory Stoneman Douglas High School in Parkland, Florida, have answered this question with their words and actions. On February 14, 2018, a former student entered their school, shooting and killing seventeen students and injuring seventeen more. In response, several students, including Emma González, Sam Zeif, David Hogg, Jaclyn Corin, Alex Wind, Kyle Kashuv, and Cameron Kasky founded a nonprofit to end gun violence through reforming gun laws.

In the days following the school shooting, Cameron Kasky said on *60 Minutes*, "We're the mass shooting generation." Kasky was born just after the mass shooting at Columbine High School in Columbine, Colorado, on April 20, 1999. But these students want to be known for ending school shootings instead of surviving this one.

Six days after the shooting, the students headed to their state capitol for a lobbying event. They gave speeches, hoping to persuade their state government to pass gun control legislation. Emma González opened her speech with these words:

> *Every single person up here today, all these people should be home grieving. But instead we are up here standing together because if all our government and president can do is send thoughts and prayers, then it's time for victims to be the change that we need to see. Since the time of the Founding Fathers and since they added the Second Amendment to the Constitution, our guns have developed at a rate that leaves me dizzy. The guns have changed but our laws have not.*

The students spearheaded the Enough! National School Walkout Day on March 14, where high school students across the country walked out of their school buildings and kept silence for seventeen minutes, one minute for each victim of the Douglas shooting.

They helped organize the March for Our Lives in Washington, DC, raising more than $4 million through GoFundMe. While planning the march, the students recognized that they had something many gun violence victims didn't have: privilege. As young people from a mostly white, affluent suburban school, they'd received more media attention and money than most anti–gun violence organizations. To repair that breach, they combined their efforts with other young activists across the country, inviting them to speak at the March for Our Lives.

After the march, the students set out on the Road to Change, a multi-community bus tour. They gave speeches and met with community leaders and the friends, family members, and survivors of gun violence. They registered more than 50,000 young people to vote.

The artist and educator **Sister Corita Kent (1918–1986)** used poetry and art to teach about social injustice. Corita incorporated the words from advertising slogans, lyrics, popular slang, and the Bible into her art. She put her art on cards, posters, and murals. She said, "Don't belittle yourself. Be BIG yourself."

They founded the group March for Our Lives to support young people in fighting for "sensible gun violence prevention policies." In 2018, they won the International Children's Peace Prize, an award that has been given since 2005 to a young person who fights courageously for the rights of children.

So we are speaking up for those who don't have anyone listening to them, for those who can't talk about it just yet, and for those who will never speak again. We are grieving, we are furious, and we are using our words fiercely and desperately because that's the only thing standing between us and this happening again.

—*Emma González*

At March for Our Lives, eleven-year-old **Naomi Wadler** **(2006–)** from George Mason Elementary School in Alexandria, Virginia, spoke to the crowd. She and her friend Carter Anderson organized a walkout at their school and added another minute of silence for a victim who had died in a school shooting in Alabama.

WRITE NOW

The students from Marjorie Stoneman Douglas High School used words to encourage voting and changes in gun laws. Create a speech, video, graphic story, or cartoon that might change how people think about or act on an important issue.

WRITE TO CREATE

Many protest signs use wordplay to make a point. Some March for Our Lives protest signs read:

> *The scariest thing in a school*
> *should be my grades.*
> *Arms are for hugging.*
> *I want to read books, not*
> *eulogies.*

Create your own protest slogans and signs. Where will you carry or post them?

Write to Write

Whether we race through the story to find out what happens next or savor every word, we know when the writer has chosen the right words. It's hard to imagine that they started with a blank page.

But they did.

What happens when you see a blank page? Do you think, "Help! I don't have any ideas!" or "I have too many ideas! I don't know where to begin!"?

How can we tackle the blank page without freaking out?

We can conquer the blank page by never facing one. Take out that paper and scribble down some words. Now, doesn't that feel better? When we brainstorm on paper, we're no longer staring at nothing. We've got a place to start forming our story, letter, or poem. Here are seven ways to "write to write" and banish the blank page forever!

MIND MAP

A mind map captures your ideas in a visual format. The process of mind mapping can help you generate, record, and organize your thoughts.

Write the topic in the center of the page. Draw lines out from the center topic, like rays around the sun, and add a category at the end of each ray. Record what you know, and brainstorm ideas. Categories might include facts, stories, images, themes, examples, statistics, and more.

MAPS

When it's time to write about your own experience, drawing a map can help you remember. Draw a map of the place you'll be writing about. Don't worry about being accurate. Instead, as you draw the map, note what you recall about what happened.

LISTS

You've written to-do lists, wish lists, and maybe even shopping lists. Next time you have a story to write, and you have no idea what to write about, make a list. Write down your ideas, questions, doubts, or anything else that will help you get started.

THE FACTS

Many writers begin the writing process by answering six questions: who, what, when, where, why, and how.

THE CHART

Create a chart to help you record and sort information. If you're writing a story, your chart might include categories like character, setting, and conflict. If you are writing a nonfiction piece, it might identify the main points and supporting data.

FREEWRITING

Write down everything you're thinking about the writing activity, even your feelings. Your freewrite can take the form of a journal entry, a letter to a friend, a story, or a list.

DRAWING

Do you think in pictures? Sketch out your ideas. Make a comic of your story. Add words later.

Write to Revise

When we compare our writing to the songs and books we love, it can be discouraging. How did they find the right words when our work sounds *meh*? We might imagine they're just smarter or more creative than we are. We might worry that our writing can never compete in the real world. And if it doesn't shine, how can it change the world?

Don't give up! Don't compare your first draft to someone else's finished product. Writing is a process, not an event. Some of the most important work you will do as a writer happens during revision. You'll streamline your message, remove unnecessary points, and find the juiciest words. Here's a short revision process to help you turn your scribbles into life-changing statements, songs, and more.

GIVE IT A REST.

Have you ever gone to bed cranky or sad and woken up feeling happier? Most of us benefit from a good night's sleep. When we've spent a lot of time on a project, it's tough to jump right into revising. Take a break from your project. That will help you approach it with fresh eyes.

REVIEW FOR CONTENT.

Read your piece, making notes about your experience. Focus on the content and how you are making your point. Don't worry about spelling, grammar, and sentence construction. You don't want to spend time fixing mistakes that will be deleted anyway. As you read, you might ask questions like:

- Does the story flow?
- Do I make my point?
- Do I use the right amount of evidence or stories?

- What works?
- What doesn't work?
- What's missing?

ASK FOR FEEDBACK.

Ask classmates or friends to read your piece and share their response to your writing. It can be helpful to guide readers by asking them to read with specific questions in mind, such as:

- What was the main idea in the story?
- How did you feel when you read it?
- What questions do you have?
- What would you like to hear more about?
- What would you like to hear less about?

REVISE.

Using your notes from your first read-through and feedback from readers, revise your piece. Remember, focus on the big picture: communicating your message and offering supporting evidence or stories. Once you've rewritten your piece and feel satisfied that it tells a good story, read it again for sentence construction, word choice, grammar, and spelling. This is your chance to spiff up your writing so your story really shines.

GET EDITED.

Ask your readers to take on the role of editor. Just like you did for yourself, they will read your story for meaning. After reading to make sure you've told a good story, they can review the story for grammar, spelling, and presentation.

Write to Advise:
Advice from Writers on Writing

**There are three rules for writing a novel.
Unfortunately, no one knows what they are.**

—W. Somerset Maugham

What rules do you follow when you write?

When George Orwell wrote the article "Why I Write," he stated his rules for writing, including: "Break any of these rules sooner than say anything outright barbarous." Many of the writers profiled in this book offered advice to other writers. Here are some of their rules.

WRITERS READ.

You use your reading not only to learn about the mechanics of writing but also to learn how other people have written to gather information that has nothing to do with your writing because everything goes into the well. And when you begin to write, it's surprising what you suddenly find coming out.

—Octavia Butler

WRITERS LEARN.

And never stop learning. Take time to read other papers, to look at what other people are doing and see what you can learn from them. There's always something new to learn as all of sports are constantly changing. And you keep up with them.

—Mary Garber

WRITERS OBSERVE.

It never occurred to me that it might be worthwhile to make my own observations and describe the experiences peculiarly my own. . . . I am resolved to be myself, to live my own life, and write my own thoughts when I have any.

—Helen Keller

WRITERS LISTEN.

I tried to write poems like the songs they sang on Seventh Street. . . . Their songs . . . had the pulse beat of the people who kept going.

—Langston Hughes

WRITERS RECORD.

When I write a story like that, I'm serving my community by telling our stories. That's the role of every writer: to serve their community, whatever it is. If you don't write it down, it's like it never happened. We're not in history as women if we don't write it down. . . . My role as a writer is to give that voice to those who don't have a voice.

—Sandra Cisneros

WRITERS EXPLORE.

When you're writing, you're trying to find out something which you don't know. The whole language of writing for me is finding out what you don't want to know, what you don't want to find out. But something forces you to anyway.

—James Baldwin

WRITERS JOURNAL.

Writing in a diary is a really strange experience for someone like me. Not only because I've never written anything before, but also because it seems to me that later on neither I nor anyone else will be interested in the musings of a thirteen-year-old schoolgirl. Oh well, it doesn't matter. I feel like writing, and I have an even greater need to get all kinds of things off my chest.

—Anne Frank

WRITERS WRITE.

I am very poorly today & very stupid & hate everybody & everything. One lives only to make blunders. . . . I am going to write a little book for Murray on orchids & today I hate them worse than everything so farewell & in a sweet frame of mind,

I am

Ever yours

—Charles Darwin

Perhaps it is just as well to be rash and foolish for a while. If writers were too wise, perhaps no books would get written at all. It might be better to ask yourself 'Why?' afterward than before. Anyway, the force of somewhere in space which commands you to write in the first place, gives you no choice. You take up the pen when you are told, and write what is commanded. There is no agony like bearing an untold story inside you.

—Zora Neale Hurston

What can I share with the younger generation of Black women writers, writers in general? What can they learn from my experience? I can tell them not to be afraid to feel and not to be afraid to write about it. Even if you are afraid, do it anyway. We learn to work when we are tired; so we can learn to work when we are afraid.

—Audre Lorde

WRITERS PERSIST.

Talent is insignificant. I know a lot of talented ruins. Beyond talent lie all the usual words: discipline, love, luck, but, most of all, endurance.

—James Baldwin

WRITERS REVISE.

Given the initial talent . . . writing is largely a matter of application and hard work, of writing and rewriting endlessly, until you are satisfied that you have said what you want to say as clearly and simply as possible. For me, that usually means many, many revisions.

—Rachel Carson

WRITERS WRITE NOW.

And it's never too early to start if you are interested in newspaper work. You can start when you're in grammar school, as far as that goes. And you can certainly start in high school.

—Mary Garber

What are your rules for writing?

Writers Read

A Writer's Notebook: Unlocking the Writer Within You by Ralph Fletcher

Courageous Creativity: Advice and Encouragement for the Creative Life
by Sara Zarr

*Create Your Own Graphic Novel: A Guide for Kids: Write and Draw Your Own
Book* by David Wayne Chiu

How to Write a Great Story by Caroline Lawrence

Making Books with Kids: 25 Paper Projects to Fold, Sew, Paste, Pop, and Draw
by Esther K. Smith, illustrated by Jane Sanders, art by Dikko Faust

Rip the Page! Adventures in Creative Writing by Karen Benke

Secrets of Storytelling: A Creative Writing Workbook for Kids
by Natalie Rompella

Spilling Ink: A Young Writer's Handbook by Ellen Potter and Anne Mazer,
illustrated by Matt Phelan

What Is Poetry? The Essential Guide to Reading and Writing Poems
by Michael Rosen

*Write Your Own Haiku for Kids: Write Poetry in the Japanese Tradition - Easy
Step-by-Step Instructions to Compose Simple Poems* by Patricia Donegan

Writing Radar: Using Your Journal to Snoop Out and Craft Great Stories
by Jack Gantos

Acknowledgments

This book began in a writing class I offered for a small group of teenaged girls. We listened to Nina Simone's "Young, Gifted and Black" and read Langston Hughes's poems. I watched the teens' eyes light up as they wrote about their own dreams for the future. By the end of the class, they had named themselves the "Dream Keepers"—and asked to keep reading and writing together.

I'm deeply grateful to the many people who supported the creation of *Mightier Than the Sword*. Andrew DeYoung discovered my #PitMad pitch and gave *Mightier* a home at Beaming Books. My editors Jill Braithwaite and Elizabeth Schleisman offered insightful guidance from beginning to end. Heidi Mann's keen eye helped make the prose clearer. The diversity readers Lynn Brown and Maria del Carmen Cortéz provided thoughtful comments so that the book's culturally diverse stories were presented more accurately. Melina Ontiveros turned this book into a work of art with her amazing illustrations.

I owe a huge debt of gratitude to my first readers. Harold Eppley, Jane Kelley, and Eliana Melander-Eppley read early drafts of the book proposal and chapters and gave me wise counsel. My SCBWI colleagues Jerrianne Hayslett, Kira Bigwood, Laurel Klein, and Sandy Brehl read chapters and offered helpful advice. Several people provided specific advice and information or pointed the way to resources, including Dr. Ross E. Dunn, Rebekah Eppley, Elizabeth Gabriel, Enid Gruszka, and Emily Stueven. These and other friends—too many to name—encouraged me through the long process of researching, writing, and pitching this book.

I'm thankful for the many organizations who have supported the Dream Keepers and my work as a teaching artist. I received expert training and guidance from Elise Riepenhoff and Jim Vopat of the National Writing Project. The Milwaukee Public Library, Arts at Large, the Milwaukee Art Museum, Hephatha Lutheran Church, and Urban Roots Freedom School welcomed and championed my work with young people. The many students I've worked with over the years opened up their hearts and told their stories—making me a better teacher and this a better book.

In the past year, my colleagues and students at Milwaukee Area Technical College have inspired me. My Write Now! Coach clients, especially the Writing Goddesses, have cheered me on. And the Milwaukee County Federated Library System generously allowed me to check out more than one hundred books at a time so that I could research and write this book in the midst of the global pandemic.

Most of all, I'm grateful to my family. From the beginning, my parents, Diane and Dick Melander, handed me books and paper and encouraged me to read and write. My mother-in-law, Linda Eppley, shared stories that piqued my curiosity to learn more. My husband, Harold Eppley, listened to me tell stories about the people in this book and cooked for me every single night. My children, Samuel and Eliana, nudged me to get out of my office and into the world. My canine companions, Maisie and Max, provided endless laughs and cuddles.

And thanks to you, dear reader—for finding this book, reading the stories, and writing about your hopes and dreams. You will write to change the world!

Rochelle Melander is a speaker, a professional certified coach, and the founder of Dream Keepers, a writing workshop that encourages young people to write about their lives and dreams for the future. Rochelle wrote her first book at seven and has published eleven books for adults. *Mightier Than the Sword* is her debut book for children. She lives in Milwaukee, Wisconsin.

Melina Ontiveros is a Mexican artist and illustrator. As a proud self-taught artist, she enjoys experimenting with color and textures in her pieces. She's currently working as a full-time freelance book illustrator, excited to bring new (and also old) stories to life, always with an open mind to learn new things during the process.

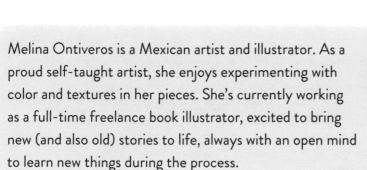

Quotation Sources

Introduction. "The pen is mightier than the sword" from *Richelieu: or, The Conspiracy: A Play, in Five Acts* by Edward Bulwer-Lytton (London: Saunders and Otley, Conduit Street, 1839), p. 39. Retrieved November 3, 2020, via Internet Archive; "Four hostile newspapers…" in *Oxford Essential Quotations* edited by Susan Radcliffe (Oxford University Press, online version, 2018) DOI: 10.1093/acref/9780191866692.001.0001. Retrieved November 3, 2020; "The word is mightier…" from Ahiqar in Wikipedia, s.v., "The Pen is Mightier than the Sword," last modified October 10, 2020, https://en.wikipedia.org/wiki/The_pen_is_mightier_than_the_sword Retrieved November 3, 2020; "Intense gunfire…" and other tweets from Rene Silva https://www.bbc.com/news/world-latin-america-11862593 Retrieved November 4, 2020.

Murasaki Shikibu. "Just my luck! What a pity" from *The Diary of Lady Murasaki* by Murasaki Shikibu, translated by Richard John Bowring (New York: Penguin, 1996), p. 58; "What kind of lady…" *The Diary of Lady Murasaki*, p. 55; "People who think so much…" *The Diary of Lady Murasaki*, p. 54; "I was all impatience…" from *The Sarashina Diary* by Anonymous in *Diaries of Court Ladies of Old Japan* translated by Annie Shepley Omori and Kochi Doi, with an introduction by Amy Lowell (Boston and New York: Houghton Mifflin Company, 1920), p. 18; "Wicked, indeed," *The Diary of Lady Murasaki*, p. 126.

Abu Abdullah Muhammad Ibn Battuta. "Swayed by…" *The Travels of Ibn Battutah*, edited by Tim Mackintosh-Smith (New York: Macmillan's Collector's Library, 2016), p. 3; "If God decrees my death…" *Ibn Battuta: Travels in Asia and Africa 1325-1354*, tr. and ed. H. A. R. Gibb (London: Broadway House, 1929), p. 11; "I was so affected…" Gibb, p. 43; "Traveling—it leaves you…" https://www.goodreads.com/quotes/508820-traveling-it-leaves-you-speechless-then-turns-you-into-a-storyteller Retrieved November 4, 2020.

Martin Luther. "What if that was the devil calling you?" *Martin Luther* by Martin Marty (New York: Viking, 2004), p. 10; "If you want to change the world, pick up your pen and write." https://www.goodreads.com/quotes/83789-if-you-want-to-change-the-world-pick-up-your

William Shakespeare. "Too much of a good thing…" Shakespeare, *As You Like It*, Act 4, Scene 1; "Laughingstock." Shakespeare, *The Merry Wives of Windsor*, Act 3, Scene 1; "It's Greek to me." Shakespeare, *Julius Caesar*, Act 1, Scene 2; "The cause of plagues is sin…" *Politics and the Paul's Cross Sermons, 1558-1642* by Mary Morrissey (Oxford: Oxford University Press, 2011), p. 82; "A plague on both your houses." Shakespeare, *Romeo and Juliet*, Act 3, Scene 1; "There is an upstart Crow…" E. A. J. Honigmann. "Tiger Shakespeare and Gentle Shakespeare." *The Modern Language Review* 107, no. 3 (2012): 699–711. Accessed June 10, 2020. DOI: 10.5699/modelangrevi.107.3.0699, p. 699; "He was not of an age but for all time!" from "To the Memory of My Beloved the Author, Mr. William Shakespeare" by Ben Jonson https://www.poetryfoundation.org/poems/44466/to-the-memory-of-my-beloved-the-author-mr-william-shakespeare; "She Phebes me." Shakespeare, *As You Like It*, Act 4, Scene 3; "Come, sermon me no further." Shakespeare, *Timon of Athens*, Act 2, Scene 2; "Disorder, that hath spoil'd us, friend us now!" Shakespeare, *Henry V*, Act 4, Scene 5; "Thou leathern-jerkin, crystal-button…" Shakespeare, *Henry IV* Part 1, Act 2, Scene 4; "Tomorrow and tomorrow…" Shakespeare, *Macbeth*, Act 5, Scene 5; "Suit the action to the word," Shakespeare, *Hamlet*, Act 3, Scene 2.

Write to Film: Screenplays. "Company F, 1st Ohio Volunteers…" https://www.loc.gov/item/98501030/; "If you can dream it, you can do it." https://www.goodreads.com/quotes/24673-if-you-can-dream-it-you-can-do-it-always; "You have many years ahead of you…" https://nofilmschool.com/Steven-Spielberg-Quotes. "That's why I…" https://www.slashfilm.com/the-matrix-trans-allegory/

Maria Merian. "From youth on I have been occupied with the investigation of insects." *The Girl who Drew Butterflies: How Maria Merian's Art Changed Science* by Joyce Sidman (Boston: Houghton Mifflin Harcourt, 2018), p. 12.

Sor Juana Inés de la Cruz. "I began to pester..." *Sor Juana Inés de la Cruz, Selected Writings*, trans. Pamela Kirk Rappaport (New York: Paulist, 2005), p. 259; "Wasted much time..." Sor Juana Inés de la Cruz, *Selected Writings*, p. 251; "Book of Jesus Christ..." *Selected Writings*, p. 250; "The queen of the sciences..." *Selected Writings*, p. 261; "The second impossibility..." *Selected Writings*, p. 253; "When I say something..." *Selected Writings*, p. 285.

Phillis Wheatley. "Slender, frail female child." https://www.poetryfoundation.org/poets/phillis-wheatley Accessed November 11, 2020; "...for in every human Breast, God has implanted a Principle..." in *Phillis Wheatley: Complete Writings* edited and with an introduction by Vincent Caretta (New York: Penguin Books, 2001), p. 153; "While an intrinsic..." from "To the University of Cambridge, in New-England" in *Phillis Wheatley: Complete Writings* edited and with an introduction by Vincent Caretta (New York: Penguin Books, 2001), p. 11.

Wang Zhenyi. "I once compared my..." *Reverie and Reality: Poetry on Travel by Late Imperial Chinese Women* by Yanning Wang (New York: Lexington Books, 2013), p. 71; "I also met the talented..." *Reverie and Reality: Poetry on Travel by Late Imperial Chinese Women*, p. 71; "There were times..." *Notable Women Of China: Shang Dynasty To The Early Twentieth Century* by Barbara Bennett Peterson (New York: M.E. Sharp, 2000), pp. 341–345; "Actually, it was definitely because of the moon..." *The Unforgotten Sisters: Female Astronomers and Scientists Before Caroline Herschel* by Gabriella Bernardi (Chichester, UK: Springer Praxis Books, 2016), p. 157; "It's made to believe/Women are the same as Men..." *Notable Women Of China: Shang Dynasty To The Early Twentieth Century*, p. 345.

Sequoyah. "When a talk is made..." *The Rise and Fall of the North American Indians* by William Brandon (Lanham, Maryland, Roberts Rinehart Publishers, 2003), p. 320.

Write to Declare: The United States Declaration of Independence. "Reason first, you are a Virginian..." from John Adams to Timothy Pickering, August 6, 1822, https://founders.archives.gov/documents/Adams/99-02-02-7674; "[The] liberty of speaking and writing...guards our other liberties." Thomas Jefferson: Reply to Philadelphia Democratic Republicans, 1808. ME 16:304.

Sojourner Truth. "I sell the shadow..." *Enduring Truths: Sojourner's Shadows and Substance* by Darcy Grimaldo Grigsby (Chicago: The University of Chicago Press, 2015), p. 125; "Through God who created..." "I have heard the bible..." "Ain't I a Woman?" https://www.thesojournertruthproject.com/compare-the-speeches; "I am a self made woman..." *Narrative of Sojourner Truth* by Sojourner Truth, introduction and Notes by Imani Perri (New York: Barnes and Noble Classics, 2005), p. 3; "Truth is powerful..." *Narrative of Sojourner Truth*, p. 105.

Louis Braille. "The kingdom of the partly blind..." *Remember Laughter: A Life of James Thurber* by Neil A. Grauer (Lincoln, NE: University of Nebraska Press, 1994), p. 67; "A writer...must believe," "The Self-Portrait Jorge Luis Borges Drew After Going Blind" by Emily Temple, LitHub, August 24, 2018, https://lithub.com/the-self-portrait-jorge-luis-borges-drew-after-going-blind/; "We must be treated as equals..." https://www.mcbdds.org/305/Louis-Braille.

Charles Darwin. "You care for nothing but shooting..." *Charles Darwin* by Kathleen Krull (New York: Viking, 2010), p. 37; "I am a complete millionaire..." "Letter to J.D. Hooker," September 23, 1864, in *Charles Darwin* by Kathleen Krul, p. 15.

Ada Lovelace. "I have got a scheme..." "Innovate by Working Together: Ada Lovelace" https://www.byui.edu/information-technology/blog/innovate-by-working-together-ada-lovelace Accessed July 7, 2020; "What is imagination..." *Ada, the Enchantress of Numbers: A Selection from the Letters of Lord Byron's Daughter and Her Description of the First Computer* by Betty A. Toole (Mill Valley, CA: Strawberry Press, 1992), pp. 136–7; "The Analytical Engine..." "Celebrating Ada Lovelace" https://mitpress.mit.edu/blog/celebrating-ada-lovelace; Accessed November 11, 2020; "It can do whatever we know how to order it to perform." "Untangling the Tale of Ada Lovelace" by Stephen Wolfram, December 10, 2015, https://writings.stephenwolfram.com/2015/12/untangling-the-tale-of-ada-lovelace/ Accessed November 11, 2020; "If you can't give me poetry..." "The Poetical Science of Ada Lovelace" by Meghan Barrett, September 7, 2016, http://meghan-barrett.com/blog/2016/09/07/the-poetical-science-of-ada-lovelace/ Accessed November 11, 2020.

Frederick Douglass. "From that moment…" *Narrative of a Life of Frederick Douglass, an American Slave, Written by Himself* (New Haven, CT: Yale University Press, 2001), p. 33; "During this time, my copy-book…" *Narrative of a Life*, p. 39; "Right is of no sex…" "The North Star American Newspaper," Encyclopedia Britannica (online), November 11, 2016, https://www.britannica.com/topic/The-North-Star-American-newspaper Accessed November 11, 2020; "Bread of knowledge…" *Narrative of a Life of Frederick Douglass, an American Slave, Written by Himself* (New Haven, CT: Yale University Press, 2001), p. 36; "I felt like one…" *Narrative of a Life of Frederick Douglass, an American Slave, Written by Himself* (New Haven, CT: Yale University Press, 2001), p. 78; "In my imagination, I already saw myself…" *Frederick Douglass' Paper*, v. 5 no. 5: January 22, 1852, https://exhibits.library.pdx.edu/exhibits/show/gates/slavery-and-abolitionism/frederickdouglaspaper.html.

Write to Abolish: The Reconstruction Amendments. "Forever free" Transcript of the proclamation, https://www.archives.gov/exhibits/featured-documents/emancipation-proclamation/transcript.html; "Neither slavery…" Transcript of 13th Amendment to the U.S. Constitution: Abolition of Slavery (1865), https://www.ourdocuments.gov/doc.php?flash=false&doc=40&page=transcript; "Life, liberty…" Declaration of Independence: A Transcription, https://www.archives.gov/founding-docs/declaration-transcript; "Some man…made a little speech" *Up From Slavery: The Incredible Life Story of Booker T. Washington* By Booker T. Washington (New York: Dover Publications, 1995), p. 10; "Verily, the work…" https://www.battlefields.org/learn/biographies/frederick-douglass.

Florence Nightingale. "A thousand thanks for your bottle of ink." Letter to William Farr, December 10, 1863, http://hgar-srv3.bu.edu/web/florence-nightingale.

Ida B. Wells. "Mother, if you don't go," *Ida B. Wells: Mother of the Civil Rights Movement* by Dennis Brindell Fradin and Judith Bloom Fradin (New York: Clarion Books, 2000), p. 128; "The way to right wrongs…" https://herdacity.org/ida-b-wells/; "Brave woman!" *Ida B. Wells: Let the Truth Be To*ld by Walter Dean Myers Illustrated by Bonnie Christensen (New York: Amistad, 2008), p. 25; "Educate a woman, and you educate a family." "Overlooked No More: Jovita Idár, Who Promoted Rights of Mexican-Americans and Women" by Jennifer Medina, The New York Times, August 7, 2020; "The people must know…" https://www.bustle.com/articles/97825-ida-b-wells-8-most-badass-quotes-show-that-she-was-strong-fearless-and-all-around-amazing.

Nellie Bly. "Riotous conduct" and "wild antics" *Nellie Bly: Daredevil, Reporter, Feminist* by Brooke Kroeger (Times Books/Random House, 1994), p. 13; "monstrosity" "Nellie's Milestones" https://www.pbs.org/wgbh/americanexperience/features/world-nellie-milestones; "There they were all, without disguise…" https://www.boweryboyshistory.com/2007/10/horrors-of-roosevelt-island-lunacy.html; "I said I could and I would. And I did." *Ten Days In a Mad-House* by Nellie Bly (New York: Ian L. Munro, publisher), Chapter 1, https://digital.library.upenn.edu/women/bly/madhouse/madhouse.html.

Qiu Jin. "It's difficult to exchange a woman's headdress for a helmet." https://www.encyclopedia.com/women/encyclopedias-almanacs-transcripts-and-maps/qiu-jin-c-1875-1907; "That person's behavior is worse…" https://duerkennstmichnicht.wordpress.com/tag/china/; "I would now rouse women's essence…" Feminism and Socialism in China by Elisabeth Croll (Routledge Revivals). (New York: Taylor & Francis, 2013), p. 68; "Female knight-errant of Mirror Lake." *Chinese Women in a Century of Revolution, 1850–1950* by Ono Kazuko, edited by Joshua A. Fogel (Stanford, CA: Stanford University Press, 1978), p. 64; "Autumn rain and autumn wind." *Ch'iu Chin: A Chinese Heroine* by Lionel Giles (London: East & West, Ltd, 1917), p. 16; "leaders can speak anywhere…" Chinese Women in a Century of Revolution, 1850–1950 by Ono Kazuko, edited by Joshua A. Fogel (Stanford, CA: Stanford University Press, 1978), p. 62; "It also became my way…" https://www.teenvogue.com/story/amani-al-khatahtbeh-founder-of-muslimgirl-website; "Don't tell me women/are not the stuff of heroes" http://self.gutenberg.org/articles/eng/Qiu_Jin.

Mary McLeod Bethune. "When she said that to me," *Mary McLeod Bethune: Building a Better World Essays and Selected Documents* edited by Audrey Thomas McCluskey and Elaine M. Smith (Indiana University Press, 2002), p. 36; "peace maker" *Mary McLeod Bethune: Building a Better World Essays and Selected Documents*, p. 43; "For I am my mother's daughter…" *American Women Activists' Writings: An Anthology, 1637–2001* by Kathryn Cullen-DuPont (New York: Cooper Square Press, 2002), p. 291; "If I have a legacy to leave my people…" https://freemaninstitute.com/bethune.htm; "The whole world opened to me when I learned to read." https://www.goodreads.com/quotes/19571-the-whole-world-opened-to-me-when-i-learned-to.

Zitkála-Šá. "As each in turn began to tell a legend…" *American Indian Stories* by Zitkála-Šá Introduction by Layli Long Soldier (New York: Modern Library, 2009), p. 8; "I felt the cold blades…" *American Indian Stories* by Zitkála-Šá Introduction by Layli Long Soldier (New York: Modern Library, 2009), p. 31.; "Such worse than barbarian rudeness…" *American Indian Stories*, p. 45; "I loved best the evening meal." *American Indian Stories*, p. 6.

Helen Keller. "When I remember…" *Helen Keller: Rebellious Spirit* by Laurie Lawlor (New York: Holiday House, 2001), p. 141; "Terror invaded my flesh…" *Helen Keller: Rebellious Spirit*, p. 110; "Blindness has no limiting effect…" *Century Illustrated Monthly Magazine* (United States: Scribner & Company, 1908), p. 782; "He never made me…" *Helen Keller: A Life* by Dorothy Herrmann (New York: Alfred Knopf, A Borzoi Book, 1998), p. 168; "I observe, I feel, I think, I imagine…" *Century Illustrated*, p. 782.

Zora Neale Hurston. "Jump at the sun." *Dust Tracks on a Road: An Autobiography* by Zora Neale Hurston (New York: HarperCollins, 2006), p. 13; "I have the nerve…" Letter from Zora Neale Hurston to Countee Cullen (March 5, 1943) *Zora Neale Hurston: A Life in Letters* collected and edited by Carla Kaplan (New York: Doubleday, 2002, p. 482; "Research is formalized curiosity…" *Dust Tracks on a Road: An Autobiography* by Zora Neale Hurston (London: Hutchinson & Co., 1942) p. 91.

Langston Hughes. "I was unhappy for a long time…" *The Life of Langston Hughes: Volume II: 1914–1967, I Dream a World* by Arnold Rampersad (Oxford: Oxford University Press, 2002), p. 11; "It was like throwing a million bricks." *Langston Hughes: Poet* by Jack Rummel (Philadelphia, PA: Chelsea House, 2005), p. 32; "Hold fast to dreams…" "Dreams" in *The Dream Keeper and Other Poems by Langston Hughes*, illustrated by Brian Pinkney (New York: Alfred A. Knopf, 1994), p. 4; "I live in Harlem, New York City…" Obituary, Langston Hughes, The New York Times, May 23, 1967, https://archive.nytimes.com/www.nytimes.com/books/01/04/22/specials/hughes-obit.html; "My best poems…" https://walkcheerfullyblog.wordpress.com/2017/01/06/favorite-quotes-langston-hughes-the-big-sea.

George Orwell. "You are noticed more if you stand on your head than if you are right way up." https://www.brainpickings.org/2015/06/25/george-orwell-eric-blair-jacintha-buddicom; "Every line of…" "Why I Write" by George Orwell in *Gangrel*, No. 4, Summer 1946 at The Orwell Foundation, https://www.orwellfoundation.com/the-orwell-foundation/orwell/essays-and-other-works/why-i-write/ Accessed November 12, 2020; "My much writing…" *Observations on Experimental Philosophy* by Margaret Cavendish, edited by Eileen O'Neill (Cambridge: Cambridge University Press, 2001), p. 7; "Writing a book…" "Why I Write" by George Orwell.

Rachel Carson. "I can remember…" "The Right Way to Remember Rachel Carson" by Jill LaPore, March 19, 2018, Accessed March 5, 2020, https://www.newyorker.com/magazine/2018/03/26/the-right-way-to-remember-rachel-carson; "If there is poetry in my book…" *Lost Woods: The Discovered Writing of Rachel Carson* by Rachel Carson, edited by Linda Lear (Boston: Beacon Press, 1999), p. 91.

Mary Garber. "It's just a question…" Washington Press Club interview with Mary Garber by Diana K. Gentry, p. 37, http://www.wpcf.org/mary-garber; "Well, the high school kids…" Washington Press Club interview, p. 32; "That's Miss Mary Garber." Washington Press Club interview, p. 93; "There are good stories…" Washington Press Club interview, p. 73.

Hans and Sophie Scholl. "Adopt passive resistance…" *The White Rose: Munich 1942–1943* by Inge Scholl, translated by Arthur R. Schultz (Middletown, CT: Wesleyan University Press), p. 74; "We will not be silent." *Sophie Scholl and the White Rose* by Annette Dumbach and Jud Newborn (Oxford: Oneworld, 2006), p. 94; "What difference does…" *Sophie Scholl and the White Rose*, p. 152; "Despite all the powers…" *Sophie Scholl and the White Rose*, p. 15; "These Munich students, few or many…" *Sophie Scholl and the White Rose*, p. 183; "As I read those names…" *Sophie Scholl and the White Rose*, p. 184.

James Baldwin. "My father said, during all the years..." "James Baldwin: Pessimist, Optimist, Hero" by Holland Carter, The New York Times, January 31, 2019, https://www.nytimes.com/2019/01/31/arts/design/james-baldwin-david-zwirner-exhibition.html Accessed November 12, 2020; "In those days my mother..." *James Baldwin: Collected Essays* (New York: Library of America, 1998), http://movies2.nytimes.com/books/first/b/baldwin-essays.html; "You think your pain and heartbreak..." *James Baldwin: Voice from Harlem A Biography* by Ted Gottfried (New York: Franklin Watts, 1997), p. 22–23; "But it is part of the business of the writer..." *James Baldwin: Collected Essays* http://movies2.nytimes.com/books/first/b/baldwin-essays.html; "Go back to where you started." http://movies2.nytimes.com/books/98/03/29/specials/baldwin-fire.html; "You write in order to change the world..." https://pen.org/to-change-the-world.

Malcolm X. "Up, you mighty race..." *Malcom X: A Fire Burning Brightly* by Walter Dean Myers/Leonard Jenkins (New York: Amistad/HarperCollins Publishers, 2000), notes; "a realistic career..." *Malcom X: A Fire Burning Brightly* by Walter Dean Myers/Leonard Jenkins (New York: Amistad/HarperCollins Publishers, 2000); "I have often reflected upon" *The Autobiography of Malcolm X* with the assistance of Alex Haley (New York: Ballantine Books, 1964), p. 182; "True Islam doesn't have room..." *The Victims of Democracy: Malcolm X and the Black Revolution* by Eugene Victor Wolfenstein (Berkeley: University of California Press, 2021), p. 309; "Children have a lesson." "Malcolm X's Public Speaking Power" by Gwen Thompkins, NPR Code Switch, February 21, 2015, https://www.npr.org/sections/codeswitch/2015/02/21/387979086/malcolm-xs-public-speaking-power; "People don't realize how" *The Autobiography of Malcolm X*, p. 400.

Jan Morris. "I was three or..." *Conundrum* by Jan Morris (New York: Harcourt Brace Jovanovich, 1974), p. 3; "Cherished this..." *Conundrum*, p. 4; "The instrument played..." *Conundrum*, p. 6; "Stranger and imposter" *Conundrum*, p. 27; "For myself, I think I learnt my trade..." *Conundrum*, p. 32; "The essentialness of oneself." *Conundrum*, p. 25; "To myself I had been a woman..." *Conundrum*, p. 104; "Don't worry about rejection..." "Experience Everything: How a letter from one great writer changed the life of another" by Simon Winchester. American Scholar, December 5, 2020, https://theamericanscholar.org/experience-everything/; "I resist the idea..." in "Jan Morris: The Art of the Essay, No. 2" *The Paris Review*, Issue 143, Summer 1997; "I think this put me..." "Deserving the World: An Interview with Kacen Callendar" by Leila Jackson Broad Recognition: A Feminist Publication at Yale, http://www.broadsatyale.com/kacen-callender.

Patsy Takemoto Mink. "If I speak and write easily..." *Unbought and Unbossed* by Shirley Chisholm (Boston: Houghton Mifflin, 1970), pp. 7–8; "We have to build things that..." "Patsy Takemoto Mink's Trailblazing Testimony Against a Supreme Court Nominee" by Ellen Lee in *The Atlantic*, September 16, 2018, https://www.theatlantic.com/politics/archive/2018/09/patsy-takemoto-minks-trailblazing-testimony-against-a-supreme-court-nominee/570082/; "No person in..." https://www2.ed.gov/about/offices/list/ocr/docs/tix_dis.html.

Anne Frank. "I hope I will be able to confide everything." *Anne Frank: The Diary of a Young Girl* The Definitive Edition (New York: Bantam Books, 1991), p. 1; "When I write I can shake off all my cares." *Anne Frank*, p. 247; "Oh, to write!" *The Girl in the Diary: Searching for Rywka* from the Łódź Ghetto, https://jewishmuseummilwaukee.org/the-girl-in-the-diary-searching-for-rywka-from-the-lodz-ghetto/; "My diary became more than..." https://www.goodreads.com/author/quotes/2983735.Zlata_Filipovi_; "The nicest part..." *Anne Frank*, p. 217.

The Rev. Dr. Martin Luther King Jr. "We adopt the means..." "Martin Luther King, Jr. Nobel Lecture" December 11, 1964, https://www.nobelprize.org/prizes/peace/1964/king/lecture/; "Injustice anywhere is a threat..." *The Autobiography of Martin Luther King, Jr.* edited by Clayborne Carson (New York: Grand Central Publishing, 1998), p. 189; "An unjust law is..." *The Autobiography of Martin Luther King, Jr.*, p. 193; "I gradually gained a measure of satisfaction from the label." *The Autobiography of Martin Luther King, Jr.*, p. 198; "Never before have I written so long a letter." *The Autobiography of Martin Luther King, Jr.*, p. 203.

Audre Lorde. "I lay spread-eagled on the floor…" *Zami: A New Spelling of My Name A Biomythography* by Audre Lorde (Berkeley, CA: The Crossing Press, 1982), p. 22; "Books were where I found sustenance… " "Audre Lorde" with Nina Winter (1976) in *Conversations with Audre Lorde* edited by Joan Wylie Hall (Jackson, MS: University Press of Mississippi, 2004), p. 11; "I was a very difficult child…" Nina Winter in *Conversations*, p. 9; "People would say…" in "My Words Will Be There" with Mari Evans (1979) in *Conversations*, p. 71; "Primarily, I write for those women" *Conversations*, p. 72; "When I dare to be powerful…" https://kenyonreview.org/2016/02/audre-lorde.

Octavia Butler. "To escape loneliness…" "Octavia Butler" Biblio, https://www.biblio.com/octavia-butler/author/2908; "I was quiet, bookish…" "NPR ESSAY - UN RACISM CONFERENCE" by Octavia E. Butler, https://legacy.npr.org/programs/specials/racism/010830.octaviabutleressay.html; "I fantasized living impossible, but interesting lives…" *Parable of the Sower* by Octavia Butler (New York: Grand Central Publishing, 2000), p. 334; "Geez, I can write a better story than that!" and "Somebody got *paid* for writing that story!" "Octavia E. Butler: Persistence" in *Conversations with Octavia Butler* edited by Consuela Francis (Jackson, MS: University Press of Mississippi, 2010), p. 181; "Negroes can't be writers." *Bloodchild and Other Stories* by Octavia E. Butler (New York: Seven Stories Press, 1996, 2005), p. 127; "When I began writing science fiction…" "*VISIONS: IDENTITY; 'We Tend to Do the Right Thing When We Get Scared'*"The New York Times, January 1, 2000, https://www.nytimes.com/2000/01/01/books/visions-identity-we-tend-to-do-the-right-thing-when-we-get-scared.html; "I carried a big notebook…" "An Interview with Octavia Butler" by Charles Rowell in in *Conversations with Octavia Butler* edited by Consuela Francis (Jackson, MS: University Press of Mississippi, 2010), p. 80; "Tell stories filled with facts." "Octavia Butler: Writing Herself Into The Story" by Karen Grigsby Bates, Code Switch, July 10, 2017, https://www.npr.org/sections/codeswitch/2017/07/10/535879364/octavia-butler-writing-herself-into-the-story; "The fiction writer…" "In Praise of Samuel R. Delany" by Jordy Rosenberg, The New York Times, August 8, 2019, https://www.nytimes.com/2019/08/08/books/samuel-delany-jordy-rosenberg.html; "I just want to write," "For Reigning Fantasy Queen N. K. Jemisin, There's No Escape From Reality" by Lila Shapiro, Vulture, November 29, 2018, https://www.vulture.com/2018/11/nk-jemisin-fifth-season-broken-earth-trilogy.html; "My most important…" *Bloodchild and Other Stories* by Octavia E. Butler (New York: Seven Stories Press, 1996, 2005), p. 143.

Sandra Cisneros. "But that aloneness, that loneliness…" in "Only Daughter" by Sandra Cisneros in *A House of My Own: Stories from My Life* (New York: Vintage Books, 2015), p. 91; "Too bad there was no grade for art…" in "A Girl Called Daydreamer" by Sandra Cisneros in *A House of My Own: Stories from My Life* (New York: Vintage Books, 2015), p. 269; "Always straddling…" *Understanding Contemporary Chicana Literature* by Deborah L. Madsen (Columbia, South Carolina: University of South Carolina Press, 2001), p. 108; "I'm a translator." "At the Library with Sandra Cisneros; A Solo Traveler In Two Worlds" by Mary B. W. Tabor (January 7, 1993) *New York Times* https://www.nytimes.com/1993/01/07/garden/at-the-library-with-sandra-cisneros-a-solo-traveler-in-two-worlds.html; "a space for myself to go" *The House on Mango Street* by Sandra Cisneros (New York: Vintage, 1984), p . 108; "I don't think about tone…" in "Sandra Cisneros: Telling the Truth in Poetry and Prose: On Hybrid Storytelling and Detonating the Bombs of the Heart" by Sara Di Blas, LitHub, February 2, 2017, https://lithub.com/sandra-cisneros-telling-the-truth-in-poetry-and-prose.

Write to Illustrate: Comics and Graphic Novels. "Those stories have room for everyone," https://www.youtube.com/watch?v=sjobevGAYHQ.

Gene Luen Yang. "I stayed up nights thinking about Superman…" "Why Do Comics Matter?" by Gene Luen Yang, Horn Book Magazine, Nov/Dec2019, Vol. 95 Issue 6, p. 12–20, "With every project I've ever done," https://www.yabookscentral.com/blog/author-chat-with-gene-luen-yang-superman-smashes-the-klan-plus-giveaway-us-only; "Get in the habit of creation…." https://blog.ed.ted.com/2016/07/21/why-comics-belong-in-schools-and-more-ideas-from-graphic-novelist-gene-luen-yang.

Sonita Alizadeh. "Of all the genres..." https://scenenoise.com/Features/child-marriage-bride-afghan-rapper-sonita-alizadeh-interview-fights-endchildmarriage; "But I wish you..." https://lyricstranslate.com/en/dokhtar-foroshi-%D8%AF%D8%AE%D8%AA%D8%B1%D9%81%D8%B1%D9%88%D8%B4%DB%8C-brides-sale.html; "using rap music to empower girls of Afghanistan" https://asiasociety.org/asia-game-changers/sonita-alizadeh; "Rap, music, and poetry..." https://scenenoise.com/Features/child-marriage-bride-afghan-rapper-sonita-alizadeh-interview-fights-endchildmarriage.

Malala Yousafzai. "Sometimes it's better..." *I am Malala: The Girl Who Stood Up for Education and Was Shot by the Taliban* by Malala Yousafzai with Christina Lamb (New York: Little, Brown, and Company, 2013), p. 79; "How dare the Taliban ..." Yousafzai, p. 142; "We were scared..." Yousafzai, p. 138; "I know the importance..." Yousafzai, p. 214; "It was then I knew..." https://malala.org/malalas-story; "Books not bullets..." https://blog.malala.org/video-transcript-malalas-speech-at-the-oslo-education-summit-2015-facc051348a7; "I began to see..." Yousafzai, p. 157.

Sophie Cruz. "Let's fight for a green card." From the movie *Free Like the Birds*, https://www.mountainfilm.org/media/free-like-the-birds; "God made me like that." "Meet Sophie Cruz, 5-year-old who gave the pope a letter because she doesn't want her parents deported" by Arelis R. Hernández, The Washington Post, September 23, 2015, https://www.washingtonpost.com/news/local/wp/2015/09/23/meet-the-5-year-old-who-gave-the-pope-a-letter-because-she-doesnt-want-her-parents-deported/; "Don't forget about..." "Sophie Has Taken Us On Her Journey" by Michael Conti, Define American blog, October 7, 2016, https://www.defineamerican.com/blog/sophie; "My friends and I love..." "Meet Sophie Cruz," https://www.washingtonpost.com/news/local/wp/2015/09/23/meet-the-5-year-old-who-gave-the-pope-a-letter-because-she-doesnt-want-her-parents-deported/; "Let us fight with love." "Six-year-old girl gives inspiring speech at Women's March," The Independent, January 22, 2017, https://www.independent.co.uk/news/world/americas/sophie-cruz-six-year-old-immigration-activist-a7540581.html; "Greatness is what we do for others, not who we are," and "equality, justice, respect, peace." http://www.sanfernandosun.com/news/article_88d295f0-f97d-11e6-9c96-bf3fb9fe82f0.html; "Letters from kids like you..." "Asked and Answered: President Obama Responds to an Eight-Year-Old Girl from Flint" posted April 27, 2016, by Ken Meyer, https://obamawhitehouse.archives.gov/blog/2016/04/27/asked-and-answered-president-obama-responds-eight-year-old-girl-flint.

Write to Change: Speeches at March for Our Lives. "We're the mass shooting generation..." "60 Minutes' Profiles Student Leaders of the 'Mass Shooting Generation" by Mark Walsh, Education and the Media, March 28, 2018, https://blogs.edweek.org/edweek/education_and_the_media/2018/03/60_minutes_profiles_student_leaders_of_the_mass_shooting_generation.html; "Every single person up here." "Florida student Emma Gonzalez to lawmakers and gun advocates: 'We call BS'" by CNN Staff, February 17, 2018, https://www.cnn.com/2018/02/17/us/florida-student-emma-gonzalez-speech/index.html; "sensible gun violence prevention policies." https://marchforourlives.com/mission-story/; "Don't belittle yourself. Be BIG yourself." *We are Artists: Women who Made their Mark on the World* (London: Thames & Hudson, 2019) p. 57; "So we are speaking up for those..." https://www.seventeen.com/life/school/a19433627/emma-gonzalez-quotes.

Write to Advise. "There are three rules for writing..." https://www.goodreads.com/quotes/20171-there-are-three-rules-for-writing-a-novel-unfortunately-no; "Break any of these rules..." "Why I Write" by George Orwell in *Gangrel*, No. 4, Summer 1946 at The Orwell Foundation, https://www.orwellfoundation.com/the-orwell-foundation/orwell/essays-and-other-works/why-i-write/, Accessed November 12, 2020; "You use your reading not only to..." "An Interview with Octavia Butler" by Charles Rowell in in *Conversations with Octavia Butler* edited by Consuela Francis (Jackson, MS: University Press of Mississippi, 2010), p. 75; "And never stop learning." Washington Press Club interview with Mary Garber by Diana K. Gentry, p. 82, http://www.wpcf.org/mary-garber/; "It never occurred to me..." *Helen Keller: A Life* by Dorothy Herrmann (New York: Alfred Knopf. 1998), p. 84; "I tried to write poems like..." "Langston Hughes set poetry to a jazz beat" by Elizabeth Lund, Christian Science Monitor Online, February 28, 2002, https://www.csmonitor.com/2002/0228/p18s02-hfes.htm; "When I write a story like that, I'm serving..." "Sandra Cisneros: Listen, to Give Women the Catharsis of Being Heard and Believed" by Charley Locke in Texas Monthly (online) May 9, 2018, https://www.texasmonthly.com/the-culture/womens-voices-project-sandra-cisneros/; "When you're writing..." "James Baldwin, The Art of Fiction No. 78," interviewed by Jordan Elgraby, The Paris Review (online) Issue 91, Spring 1984, https://www.theparisreview.org/interviews/2994/the-art-of-fiction-no-78-james-baldwin; "Writing in a diary is..." *Anne Frank: The Diary of a Young Girl* The Definitive Edition (New York: Bantam, 1991), pp. 5–6; "I am very poorly today..." https://www.darwinproject.ac.uk/letter/DCP-LETT-3272.xml; "Perhaps it is just as well to be rash..." https://www.goodreads.com/quotes/883133-perhaps-it-is-just-as-well-to-be-rash-and; "What can I share with the younger generation..." in *I Am Your Sister: Collected and Unpublished Writings of Audre L*orde edited by Rudolph Byrd, by Johnnetta Betsch Cole, Beverly Guy-Sheftall (Oxford: Oxford University Press, 2009), p. 168; "Talent is insignificant." "James Baldwin, The Art of Fiction No. 78," interviewed by Jordan Elgraby, The Paris Review (online) Issue 91, Spring 1984, https://www.theparisreview.org/interviews/2994/the-art-of-fiction-no-78-james-baldwin; "Given the initial talent..." https://www.brainpickings.org/2017/08/28/rachel-carson-house-of-life-writing-loneliness/; "And it's never too early to start..." Washington Press Club interview with Mary Garber by Diana K. Gentry, p. 80, http://www.wpcf.org/mary-garber.